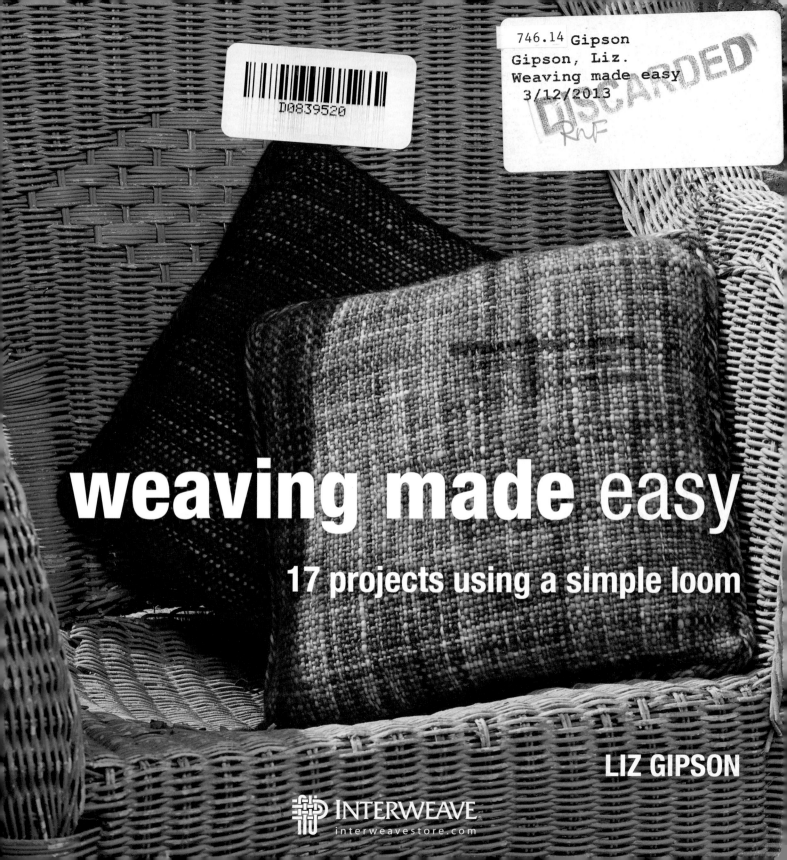

weaving made easy

17 projects using a simple loom

LIZ GIPSON

INTERWEAVE
interweavestore.com

Cover Design: Connie Poole
Interior Design: Laura Shaw
Production Design: Katherine Jackson
Technical Editing: Diane Kelly
Editing: Ann Budd
Illustrations: Gayle Ford
Photography: Joe Coca, except for the following pages by Ann Swanson:
pages 6–22, 24–59, 75, 87, 107, 115, and 119.

Interweave Press LLC
201 East Fourth Street
Loveland, CO 80537-5655 USA
interweavestore.com

Printed in China by Asia Pacific Offset.

Library of Congress Cataloging-in-Publication Data

Gipson, Liz.
  Weaving made easy : 17 projects using a simple loom /
Liz Gipson, author.
      p. cm.
  Includes index.
  ISBN 978-1-59668-075-3 (pbk.)
  1. Hand weaving. 2. Hand weaving--Patterns. 3. Handlooms. I. Title.
  TT848.G57 2008
  746.1'4041--dc22   2008014303

10 9 8 7 6 5 4 3 2

acknowledgments

To the Giants, for we all stand on their shoulders

I owe much to many. Mom and Dad provided the foundation on which I stand. My vast, extended web of family—Gipsons, Woodroofs, Howes, Heges, Tharps, and Dammans—built the framework, and my husband, Jim, helped me with the rest and was oh, so patient and encouraging during the process of constructing this particular part of our lives.

It takes a village to make a book, and I'm lucky to live in a darn great one. The book would simply not have happened if Linda Ligon hadn't meditated one day and had a vision that it should. She more than helped it along its way. Madelyn van der Hoogt gave me the encouragement, space, and support to make this book happen. Weavers and I owe her much for her dedication to the craft. Jane Patrick championed this poorly named loom after Betty Davenport lay down the torch (which she has recently picked up again, by the way). Ann Swanson is a beautiful ball of talent—from mothering to photo styling—whose inner resources are great and whose love for this loom is much appreciated.

Amy Clarke Moore, colleague and personal cheerleader, stepped in and helped with the section on color, including weaving the color samples. Judy Berndt is a model of compassion, wit, and good grammar. Liz Good, my officemate, listened to the endless chatter about this book and jumped in to reweave the Grab it and Go Bag when I ran out of time.

I am also grateful to Tricia Waddell for giving me the time to get the book right and for offering a non-weaver's perspective; Ann Budd for her consummate editing skills; Diane Kelly for consumate technical editing skills (and love of goats); Joe Coca, who is at once a fine photographer, sage, and jester; Connie Pool for loaning us her house for the photo shoot and great cover design; Laura Shaw for her clean approach to interior design; and Nancy Arndt to whom we are all grateful that her eyes cast over final pages and make them better. And finally, Marilyn Murphy, who is ceaseless in her dedication to Interweave—those of us who work here owe her more than we know.

contents

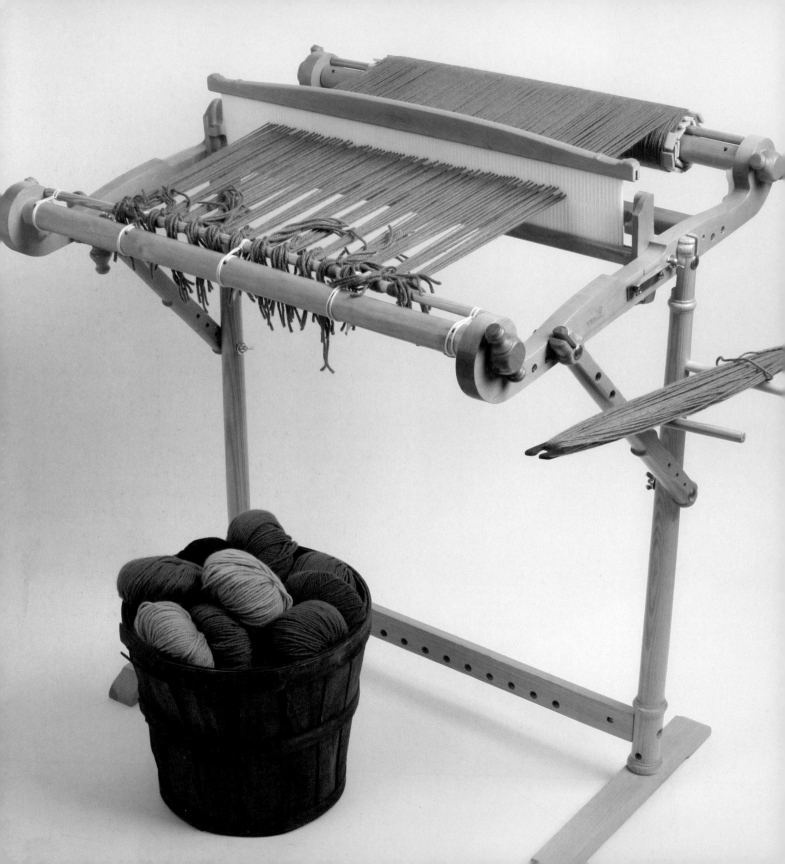

introduction

Weaving is an enchantress. I'm not sure exactly how I came under her spell. I was fortunate to learn to weave at a young age. All things fiber charmed my imagination. As a child, I would wrap my little hands around the fence surrounding the llama at the petting zoo in order to prevent my grandmother from hauling me away. I read in a book that you could weave with that llama's coat, and I wanted her to teach me how! Working with yarn simply makes me happy, and we tend to stick with things that make us happy.

Weaving, for me, is also a small act of rebellion. We are so far removed from how the items we depend on everyday—food, clothing, and shelter—are made. Now, I'm not even close to making everything I wear or all the textiles in my home, but at least I know what it takes to make the fabric that I depend on.

This little loom—the rigid heddle—is the perfect avenue for you to discover what weaving has to offer. Small and portable, it's the ideal blend of ease and functionality. Weaving is one of the fastest ways to produce cloth, and it meshes beautifully with all of your other craft skills. If you sew, you'll be in heaven creating your own fabric. If you knit or crochet, you can combine these techniques for truly unique garments. If you spin, you can create yarns for woven cloth that no one else can buy. If you have never tackled any other craft in your life, you learned all you need to know in third-grade math. Really. It's that easy!

It's time to get weaving, and this little loom is your ticket to the party.

the basics

With every new avocation comes a new vocabulary. Weaving is no exception, but fortunately, there are only a few simple terms to master. When first used, the terms are printed in boldface type; see page 122 for all terms. Woven cloth is formed when parallel yarns that are held taut are interlaced by a second yarn. As a unit, the taut yarn is called the **warp**; individual yarns (also called **threads**) are called **warp ends**. The yarn that travels over and under (or weaves) between the warp ends is called the **weft**; individual weft threads are called **picks**. Woven cloth is made by interlacing the warp ends with weft picks. Long ago, weavers came up with a variety of looms to hold the warp ends taut to facilitate interlacing them with the weft picks.

The rigid heddle is perhaps the most straightforward loom available on the market. The warp ends are threaded alternately through holes in plastic bars (**heddles**) and through the slots between the bars. As a unit, these holes and slots are called the **rigid heddle**. It is also referred to as the **beater** because it is used to "beat" the weft into place. The rigid heddle is lifted or lowered to raise or lower the warp ends to form a **shed** through which the weft is passed. Think of the shed as the space that "shelters" the weft. **Shed blocks** provide a means to hold the rigid heddle in the lifted or lowered position so both of your hands are free to manipulate the weft. The weft is most efficiently passed through the shed by means of a **stick shuttle**, a thin flat piece of wood around which the weft yarn is wrapped. By alternating sheds and beating picks of yarns, the weft yarn passes alternately over and under the warp ends to **weave** cloth.

THE RIGID HEDDLE LOOM

Cloth Beam Holds the woven cloth at the front of the loom.

Warp Beam Holds the warp threads at the back of the loom.

Shed Blocks Hold the rigid heddle in the up or down position.

Rigid Heddle Apparatus through which the warp is threaded and with which the weft yarn is "beat" or aligned perpendicular to the warp.

Front Apron Rod Where the warp is tied and tensioned at the front of the loom.

Back Apron Rod Where the warp is tied onto the back of the loom.

Reed The holes and slots in the rigid heddle.

Stand Holds the loom at a comfortable height for weaving. If you don't have a stand, prop the back of the loom on the edge of a table and rest the front in your lap.

Shed The space between adjacent warp threads through which the weft travels.

Shuttle Holds the weft.

Warp The yarns stretched on the loom.

Weft Yarn that interlaces the warp in an over-under fashion.

Brake Allows the tension of the warp to be released or tightened.

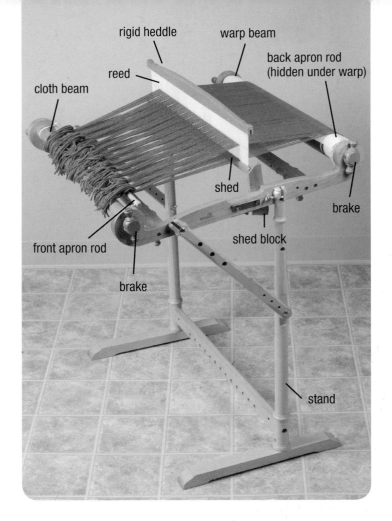

what's in a name?

Although the details are lost to time, it would have been nice if whoever named the rigid heddle loom had come up with a sexier name. Although "rigid heddle" describes the loom perfectly, it sounds so stiff and, well, rigid, for such an ingenious invention.

ACCESSORIES

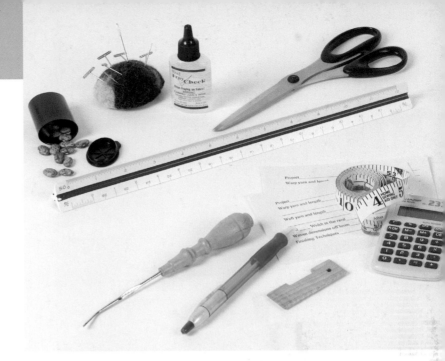

Calculator To help with the basic math needed to determine warp and weft lengths and widths, and to figure yarn amounts.

Clamps Used in conjunction with L-brackets to substitute for commercial reed stand.

Cloth tape measure Used to measure weaving progress—plan to always have one handy.

Embroidery or tapestry needle Used for finishing work and fixing mistakes.

Fray Check A liquid plastic that will safely secure woven cloth to keep it from fraying.

Heddle hook A thin flat hook with an easy-grip handle used to thread the warp yarns through the holes and slots in the rigid heddle.

Inch gauge or ruler Used to determine the thickness of yarns.

L-brackets Used to hold the rigid heddle in place while threading the warp.

Pencil or pen For taking notes as you weave.

Pick-up stick Used to manipulate the warp; also comes in handy to clear the shed when using novelty or sticky yarns in the warp.

Project planning cards or note paper For taking notes.

Reed stand A wooden stand used to prop the rigid heddle while threading the warp.

Scissors For cutting yarns.

Stick shuttle Any of a number of styles of thin flat wood that holds the weft yarn.

Tapestry beater or fork Use to beat the weft (not shown).

T-pins and small glass or plastic jars Used to mend broken warp threads.

Thick paper or warping stick Used to help maintain even tension between layers of warp rolled onto the back beam of a loom.

Warping board or peg Used to measure and organize the warp yarn in preparation for threading it on the loom.

Weighted small glass or plastic jar Used to weight a new warp end that replaces a broken one.

Yard stick Used to measure the leader yarn for the warp.

YARNS

Besides the loom, the most important tool for weaving is yarn. Until about a hundred and fifty years ago, all yarns were made from natural fibers—wool, silk, cotton, flax, yak, cashmere, and the like. Today, yarns are made from all sorts of fibers—soy, steel, bamboo, synthetics (these are nothing like your grandma's nylon), and even milk—and most are available worldwide. Add the variety of ways that these fibers can be spun and plied into yarn, and you can get a feel for the overwhelming number of choices available to weavers. To make good choices for your weaving projects, particularly which yarn to use in the warp, you'll want a general understanding of fibers and how they are spun into yarns.

Fiber Content

Wool, cotton, flax, and silk are still the most popular fibers used by weavers. Each fiber has unique properties that affect how it behaves as cloth. Properly spun, any of them will hold up under tension as a warp yarn. They can be used alone or combined with other fibers in the weft as long as the yarn produces the drape and feel (called **hand**) that you like.

Wool is a protein fiber that is technically defined by its structure, which consists of wavy or crimpy fibers that are covered with microscopic scales (as opposed to "hair," which doesn't have any scales). The word "wool" is commonly used to refer to the fiber shorn from sheep. The scales on wool fiber make it easy to spin and allows the fiber to hold the twist once spun. The crimp creates air pockets that provide elasticity and insulating properties. Wool yarn "blooms" or swells beautifully during washing. It wicks moisture and provides excellent drape. Llamas, goats, alpaca, and rabbits also produce protein fibers with properties similar to sheep's wool.

Cotton is a cellulose fiber derived from the bolls of the cotton plant. It has high durability but little elasticity, making it an excellent choice for warp. Unlike wool, cotton fibers have no crimp and produce fabrics that are more cool than insulating. In general, cotton is also highly absorbent; however, cotton yarns that have been mercerized (immersed in a bath of sodium hydroxide) have added sheen and are easier to dye but are less absorbent.

Flax, also a cellulose fiber, is made from the flax plant. It has very little elasticity but more sheen than cotton due to a higher content of wax. Flax is very strong and highly absorbent, yet it dries quickly. Yarn spun from flax fibers is called "linen." Linen is considered a luxury fiber and creates cloth that has a cool, crisp feel with beautiful drape.

Silk is a protein fiber that is made from the cocoon of the silk worm. Silk is lustrous, strong, and can take on almost one-third its weight in water without feeling wet, but in doing so, its strength decreases. Throughout history, silk has been one of the most sought after luxury fibers for its luster and drape, making it also perhaps the most mimicked fiber in history. Since the industrial revolution, textile chemists have tried to create artificial silk. Their first success was rayon and that has given rise to the much more eco-friendly Tencel, bamboo, and other silk-like yarns generated from natural materials.

dreaming in yarn

Do you see yarn and instantly have a vision of what it will be? Have you ever carried out that vision and had it turn out differently from how you imagined? Vision with a bit of experience is the key to making the cloth you want. To do this, it pays to learn a bit about how yarns are made. By learning to spin, I was able to greatly improve my intuitive knowledge on how yarns behave. But just a little bit of book learning about how yarns are made will help steer you in the right direction.

Yarn Construction
Singles and Plies

Fiber can be spun into yarn of varying thicknesses. A single strand of spun fiber is called a **singles** (note that the plural is used even when talking about a single strand of yarn). Don't be fooled into thinking that all singles are created equal—a singles can range from very fine (appropriate for weaving at 24 **ends per inch**, for example) to very thick (appropriate for weaving at 4 ends per inch, for example). A **plied yarn** is made by twisting (or plying) two or more singles together. A two-ply yarn is made up of two singles, a three-ply yarn is made up of three singles, a four-ply yarn is made up of four singles, and so on. It's important to note that the number of plies does not necessarily dictate the size of the yarn—a two-ply yarn made up of thick singles can be fatter than a six-ply yarn made up of thin singles.

Generally speaking, the more plies, the stronger the yarn. Therefore, singles typically don't make good warp yarns. Because they don't have the added

finding balance

Weavers often talk about **balanced plain weave** or **balanced weave**. In a balanced weave, the number of threads in an inch of warp is equal the number of threads in an inch of weft. If there are more threads per inch in the warp than in the weft, the fabric is said to have a **warp-emphasis weave**. On the other hand, if there are more threads per inch in the weft than in the warp, the fabric has a **weft-emphasis weave**. If the warp completely covers the weft, the fabric is called **warp dominant**; if the weft completely covers the warp, it's called **weft dominant**. The key to these types of fabrics is the spacing of the warp ends.

strength imparted by plying, singles are more susceptible to abrasion from the heddles. Smooth multi-ply yarns generally make the best warp.

Yarn can also be plied to create various novelty effects. Novelties and "sticky" yarns such as bouclé and mohair tend to cling together when forming a shed and can make the weaving process fussy. However, if these yarns are spaced wide enough apart that they don't touch each other, or if sticky yarns are alternated with smooth yarns, they can produce interesting results in the warp.

Yarn Classification

Yarns marketed for knitters are classified based on the **grist**, or size of the yarn—from laceweight at the fine end to very bulky at the thick end. Years ago, *Spin-Off* magazine compiled a chart relating yarn classification and approximate yards per pound based on a variety of sources, as well as the editor's personal experience. It's worth noting that none of the sources precisely agreed. However, the chart does provide guidelines for how knitting yarns are classified.

Yarn Classification and Yardage per Pound	
Yarn Style	**Yards/Pound**
Lace	2,600 (2,377 meters)+
Fingering	1,900–2,400 (1,737–2,195 meters)
Sport	1,200–1,800 (1,097–1,646 meters)
Worsted	900–1,200 (823–1,097 meters)
Bulky	600–800 (549–732 meters)
Very Bulky	400–800 (366–549 meters)

Yarns manufactured for weavers are classified by size, but they are often expressed by the **count system**, which is based on how many yards are in a pound of yarn of a standard size. This system was designed for industry and not the handcrafter, so it can seem a bit archaic. Each fiber type—cotton, linen, wool—had its own standards that were determined by the trade that controlled that yarn's production. Weaving yarns (often sold on cones) are typically classified by a ratio of two numbers—the numerator represents the size of the yarn with 1 being the thickest, and the denominator represents the number of plies. For example, a cotton yarn classified as 10/2 will have a thickness of "10" and be comprised of two plies. If you know the yardage for the standard size "1" of cotton (which happens to be 840 yards [768 m]/pound), you can find the yards per pound of 10/2 cotton by multiplying the two numbers together: 840 yards [768 m] per pound × 10/2 = 4,200 yards [3840 m] per pound. Fortunately, most retailers market these yarns with both the count system and yards per pound clearly labeled, so you don't have to remember any standards or do these calculations.

Warp

Now that you understand the fundamentals of yarn production, you're ready to choose yarns for your weaving project. The yarns that are held under tension on the loom are called the warp. Yarns that make the best warp are relatively smooth and tightly plied so that they will hold up under tension and endure the abrasion of the rigid heddle as it moves up and down the warp. Yarns that are fuzzy or loosely spun will tend to fray and break.

To test if a yarn will hold up under tension in a warp, pinch each end of 4- to 6-inch (10 to 15 cm) length between a thumb and index finger and pull your hands apart to create a moderate amount of even tension on the yarn. Then pull your hands apart quickly to "snap" the yarn a few times. If the yarn breaks or pulls apart in your hands, it will probably do the same when put under tension on the loom. Next, hook a bobby pin over the yarn and rub the bobby pin back and forth to mimic the friction caused by the yarn traveling through the rigid heddle. If the bobby pin causes the yarn to pill or shred, the rigid heddle will likely do so as well. But don't despair if you've fallen in love with this particular yarn—you can still use it in the weft, which undergoes much less tension and friction.

Sett

Once you've determined if a particular yarn is suitable for the warp, you'll need to decide how close to space the individual ends in the heddle. The spacing of warp ends in the heddle is called the **sett**. There are three factors that affect the sett of a warp—the number of warp ends threaded in one inch of warp, the size of the yarn used for the warp, and how the densely the weft is beat or packed in. While the spacing of the yarns is fixed by the number of slots and holes per inch in the rigid heddle (which, for most rigid heddle looms come in spacings of 5, 8, 10, 12, and 15 per inch), you have a lot of leeway in the size of the yarn you choose to use and how firmly it is beat. First, let's look at how to determine the sett or **ends per inch (epi)** of a yarn.

Determining EPI

To determine if a given yarn will give a sett for balanced weave in the size of rigid heddle that you have, wrap the yarn around a ruler for the distance of one inch (2.5 cm). Here's where an inch gauge comes in handy. The notch in an inch gauge measures exactly one inch wide. Wrap the yarn around the gauge for the length of the notch,

Wrap yarn around the notch in an inch gauge to determine the number of warps and wefts for a balanced weave.

lightly tensioning the yarn and allowing the threads to touch one another, but not overlap.

Because cloth is made up of both vertical threads (warp) and horizontal threads (weft), the number of wraps represents the sum of the two. To get the number of warp ends required for an inch of balanced plain weave, divide the number of wraps by two. This is the number of ends per inch, and it usually has a margin error of plus or minus one thread.

For example, let's say you've spotted the perfect sportweight two-ply wool at your local yarn shop. Before you head to the checkout counter, ask if you can unwind about a yard of the yarn (most yarn shops will allow you to do this as long as you wind it back onto the ball when you're done). Pull out about a yard of yarn and wrap it around your inch gauge, winding with even tension and so that the wraps just touch each other without overlapping. Let's say that you were able to wind this yarn 19 times around your inch gauge. The balanced plain-weave sett for this yarn is therefore 19 ÷ 2, or 9.5. Using the margin of error of plus or minus 1, you'll know that this yarn is suitable for balanced weave when threaded through a heddle that has 10 spacings per inch.

If, for some reason you're not able to wind the yarn on an inch gauge, you can determine the appropriate sett if you know the yards per pound of the yarn. The ball band on the ball or skein of yarn will report the number of yards (or meters) and the weight of the ball or skein. With some simple calculations, you can convert this information to yards per pound. For example, let's say the ball band on that perfect sportweight wool reports that there are about 184 yards in 1¾ ounces. (If the yarn weight is listed in grams instead of ounces—which is quite common with yarns targeted for knitting—you'll have to first convert the number of grams to ounces; there are about 28.5 grams in an ounce.) To

Common Yardages and Setts			
Yarn	yd/lb	m/kg	Sett for balanced plain weave
20/2 wool	5,600	11,300	24
3-ply laceweight wool/silk	5,040	10,150	24
3/2 cotton	1,260	2,535	14
2-ply wool	1,800	3,630	12
2-ply sportweight wool	1,488	3,000	10
4-ply cotton	840	1,605	8

determine the number of yards per pound, convert the number of ounces from fractions to decimals (i.e., 1¾ = 1.75). Divide the number of ounces in a pound (i.e., 16) by this number to get the weight, in pounds, of the ball: 16 ÷ 1.75 = 9.14 (rounding up the nearest tenth). Multiply this number by the number of yards in the skein to get the number of yards per pound: 9.14 × 184 = 1,681.

By itself, this number isn't much help. But thankfully, weavers before us calculated the appropriate setts for a range of yards per pound in a handy chart that outlines the approximate yards per pound (and typically meters per kilogram as well), fiber type and construction, and a suggested sett for that yarn. For this book, we will focus only on setts for balanced plain weave. An excerpt from the sett chart provided at the back of the book is shown above.

Notice that the chart lists yarns with different yardages as having the same sett. Some of this has to do with the how the yarn is spun or the fibers it contains—yarns of the same size can have different weights depending on the number of plies, how tightly it's spun, and the differing weights of the fibers.

Our yardage of 1,681 falls between a 2-ply wool at 1,488 yards/pound that's listed as having a balanced plain weave sett of 10 and a 2-ply wool at 1,800 yards/pound that's listed as having a sett of 12. Right away, we can tell that our yarn will work between 10 and 12 ends per inch. Although we don't know the ideal sett (for that we'd want to get a hold of a ball of yarn and count the wraps on an inch gauge), at least we have a narrow range to work with. To help narrow down the possible ranges you'd calculate for the yarns used in this book, I've provided a sett chart on page 125.

Also when thinking about sett, consider the fiber and preparation of the yarn. Wool yarns spun with lots of air will bounce back after they're released from tension from the loom, while cotton yarns won't. Setting a yarn looser than recommended for balanced plain weave will result in a lacy fabric, while yarns sett denser than recommended plain weave will be sturdier. Loose setts are recommended if you want the yarn to full or felt.

If you shop for yarns online or from catalogs that cater to weavers, you'll find that many will include information on each yarn's sett and suitability as a warp. Keep in mind, though, that warp suitability is usually based on the amount of friction caused on shaft looms,

which is typically much higher than that caused by rigid heddle looms, and many yarns labeled as unsuitable for warp may be just fine on these gentler looms. If you're in doubt, call or e-mail the yarn source to ask their opinion.

Weft

Warp yarns are just half the equation when it comes to creating great cloth. How the warp and weft interact will determine the look and feel of your cloth. If you sett for balanced plain weave and use the same yarn in the warp and weft, then the resulting cloth will have a balanced weave. Balanced weaves are just one of the ways that you can sett your yarns to get cloth. For instance, widely spaced setts with thick wefts and a strong beat will produce a sturdy rug-like fabric, while a thin weft in the same sett and a light beat will produce drapey lace.

I usually recommend adding ten inches of warp to a project so that it's possible to sample with various weft yarns. (*Note:* For economy or other reasons noted, not all the projects in this book call for sampling.) This way, if the yarn you chose for the weft doesn't seem to do the job, you can experiment with other yarns. It is much easier to swap out weft yarns than it is to rewarp the loom.

Remember that beat also plays a role in how your cloth will turn out. See "Find Your Beat" on page 42 for more information.

These swatches show how various weft colors (shown as yarn butterflies) look against the same yellow warp.

Color in Weaving

Many weavers feel adrift when it comes to selecting colors for a project. We choose colors every day of our lives—while selecting the clothes we wear or determining how to decorate our homes. Yet, choosing yarns for weaving cloth can seem daunting because it's often difficult to envision how two or more colors will interact with each other in the over-under structure of woven cloth. Unlike the simple pairing of a light blue top with brown pants, where each color is seen independently,

pairing a light blue warp with a brown weft, where the two interact with each other on a smaller scale and visually blend together, can produce a completely different color. A quick test to see how colors will react in woven fabric is to twist a strand of each together.

I often choose colors with high contrast because they show the interlacements of the warp and weft most clearly. But creating contrast is just the tip of the color theory iceberg. Entire books are published on this sub-

we all can be Vera Wang

I used to find the term "designer" both intimidating and pretentious. According to *Webster's,* the first definition of design is "to conceive in the mind." Well, that's not so daunting. Every time I see beautiful cloth, I think of how I can weave something similar on my loom. The second definition is "to form a plan." Ah, ha! All it takes to design great cloth is to have a vision and make a plan. We can all do that!

ject, but to be honest, only by weaving the yarns together will you be able to know exactly how they interact. To get a better grasp on how colors work together, try weaving a color sampler, like my friend and colleague Amy Clarke Moore did for the samples on page 19.

Amy chose twenty-six colors of Brown Sheep's Lamb's Pride Worsted yarn sett at 10 epi to weave small blocks of color against a solid yellow warp. She began with the three primary colors—red, yellow, and blue. Then she added value contrast to the mix by weaving one tint (addition of white) and one tone (addition of black) of each primary color. She then moved on to the secondary colors—green, purple, and orange—and wove one tint and one tone of each of these. Finally, Amy used the neutrals brown and gray, and wove one tint and one tone of each of brown and gray in addition to black and white.

I encourage you to weave similar samples for your own reference on how colors interact with one another in woven cloth. Refer to them when choosing colors for your next warp and weft, and you'll have a pretty good idea of what to expect.

PROJECT PLANNING

Once you have decided what you want to weave and you have selected the perfect yarn, you're ready to figure out how much yarn you'll need for the warp and weft. The amount depends on the length and width of the finished piece, plus extra to account for the yarns traveling in an over-under pattern instead of in a straight line, and extra to account for the yarn being tied on the loom. For an example, let's say that you want to use that lovely sportweight wool used in the example on page 16 to make a scarf with a finished measurement of 60" (152.5 cm) long by 6" (15 cm) wide. A scarf is a good first project because the final dimensions aren't critical—it won't be a problem if the scarf ends up a little shorter or longer.

Determine Amount of Warp

You've already determined that this sportweight yarn will weave a balanced cloth if sett at 10 ends per inch. But, before you'll know how much yarn to buy, you'll need to know how long each warp end will need to be and the total number of warp ends.

Warp Length

For a 60" (152.5 cm) finished length, it follows that the warp will need to be at least 60" (152.5 cm) long. But that's not all. You'll also need to allow extra length for the process of weaving and for attaching the warp to the loom (called warping or dressing the loom). **Take-up** includes the extra inches "taken up" as the warp threads bend over and under the weft threads (they don't travel in a straight line), the amount the fabric relaxes when it is released from tension on the loom, and the amount the fabric will shrink when it is first washed. Most weavers add an additional 10% for take-up when calculating warp length.

Loom waste is the amount of yarn needed to secure the warp ends onto the loom. It's length that can't be woven into the project, although it can be used for fringe at each end. Each loom is different, but in general, 24" (61 cm) is sufficient allowance for loom waste on a rigid heddle loom. This 24" (61 cm) allows for 6" (15 cm) to tie the yarn onto the back of the loom, 6" (15 cm) to tie the yarn onto the front of the loom, and about 6" (15 cm) at each end between where the yarn is tied on and a suitable shed can be made for weaving.

In addition, it's a good idea to allow a little extra yarn so you can weave a sample at the beginning of your project. This is a good opportunity to try out different weft yarns or finishing techniques, especially washing. For example, you can see how the sample reacts to machine washing without inadvertently ruining the woven scarf in the machine. In most cases, 10" (25.5 cm) is an adequate allowance for sampling. This amount will allow for about 5" (12.5 cm) of warp for weaving your sample; the other 5" (12.5 cm) is used to separate the sample from the beginning of your project.

For our example, the total warp length is the sum of woven length, take-up, loom waste, and sampling length:

60" (woven length of project) + 6" (10% take-up) + 24" (loom waste) + 10" (sampling allowance) = 100" total length of each warp thread.

Determine Number of Warp Ends

Next, you need to know how many warp ends you'll need to get the desired 6" (15 cm) finished width. You've already determined that you want a sett of 10 ends per inch (epi). But you'll also need to take into account widthwise take-up. In general, 10% is appropriate for take-up.

The total number of warp ends is the sum of the woven width plus take-up multiplied by the sett. For our example:

6" (woven width of project) + 0.6" (10% take-up) = 6.6" (width in the reed).
6.6" (width in reed) × 10 (sett in warp ends per inch) = 66 warp ends total.

Total Amount of Warp Yarn

Now it's a simple matter of multiplying the total length by the number of ends to get the total warp length needed:

100" (total warp length) × 66 (total warp ends) = 6,600".

To convert the number of inches to the number of yards, divide this number by 36:
6,600" ÷ 36" = 184 yards (168 m) of warp needed.

Weft

To determine the amount of yarn needed for weft, you'll need to know if you want to weave a balanced, warp-dominate, or weft-dominate cloth. For our example, let's say we want a balanced weave. By definition, there will be as many weft threads—called **picks per inch** (abbreviated **ppi**)—as warp threads. To calculate the amount of weft, multiply the width of the warp in the reed by the picks per inch and the total woven length:

6.6" (width of warp in reed) × 10 (picks per inch) × 60" (total length of woven warp) = 3,960".

To convert the number of inches to yards, divide this number by 36:
3,960" ÷ 36 = 110 yards (100 m) of weft needed.

yarn calculation tips

- Take a photocopy of the project planning worksheet (page 124) and a calculator with you when you're choosing yarn for a project. That way, you'll have no trouble determining how much yarn you'll need.

- It's a good idea to add an extra 10% to your calculations for a comfort cushion.

- If you plan to felt or full your project, increase the take-up percentage in your calculations to 30%.

- If it's important to be precise with the finished dimensions of your project and you're at all unsure about the amount of yarn to allow for take-up, loom waste, or shrinkage, test-weave a sample on a short warp before you begin your project in earnest.

warping and weaving

Once you know how much yarn you need, it's a simple matter of getting those yarns on the loom. This involves measuring and cutting the appropriate number of warp ends, threading the rigid heddle, and tying the warp on to the back apron rod and winding it on the loom under even tension. From there it's a matter of crossing those warp yarns with a separate weft yarn in an over-under-over progression to form cloth.

Don't be surprised if you feel awkward and clumsy the first few times you try it. Just like learning to ride a bike, you need to practice to get the hang of it. And don't get frustrated if you make mistakes. Even seasoned weavers make mistakes from time to time. Fortunately, most mistakes can be overcome with a few small adjustments that you'll find on page 48.

WARPING THE LOOM

Before you can weave cloth, the loom has to be "dressed." **Dressing the loom** is the process of measuring the warp, threading it through the rigid heddle, winding it onto the back beam, and putting it under uniform tension. Although there are a lot of steps, you'll find that they go quickly and it won't be long before you're able to warp an eight-inch-wide scarf in an hour or less. For easy reference, use the warping checklist on page 123.

Measuring the Warp

While it's possible to measure each warp end separately, it would take a long time, and the individual lengths would tangle hopelessly with each other. Fortunately, there are a variety of ways to make this easier. The method I like best uses a **warping board**. A warping board consists of a number of pegs attached to a square frame. Some rigid heddle looms have built-in warping boards. If yours doesn't, consider purchasing one. Many looms also include warping pegs, which can substitute for a warping board. Warping pegs can be clamped to surfaces that are spread apart the distance of the desired warp length, then the warp can be wound between them. They even allow you to wind your warp and thread the rigid heddle simultaneously. But in all my years of teaching, I find that warping boards are easier for beginning weavers.

To begin, place the warping board at a comfortable height—I have mine mounted on the wall, but you can also place it on a narrow tabletop and prop it against the wall. Let's use the scarf project from the previous section for our warping example. We calculated that the warp ends will need to be 100" (254 cm) long and that we'll need 66 of them. The first step is to measure the 100" length with a **leader yarn**. The leader yarn is any inelastic yarn, such as thick cotton, that won't stretch

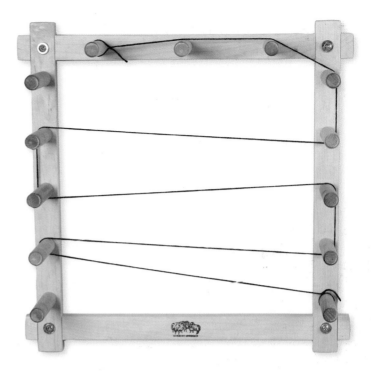

Beginning at the top left, zig and zag the leader yarn as necessary to end at a peg.

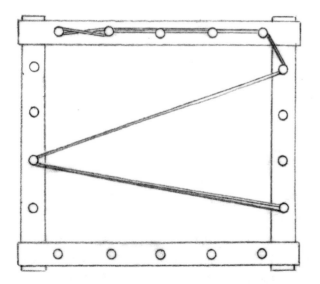
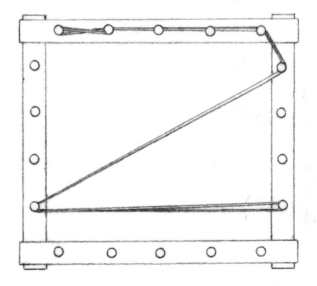

Two possible paths for a three-yard warp.

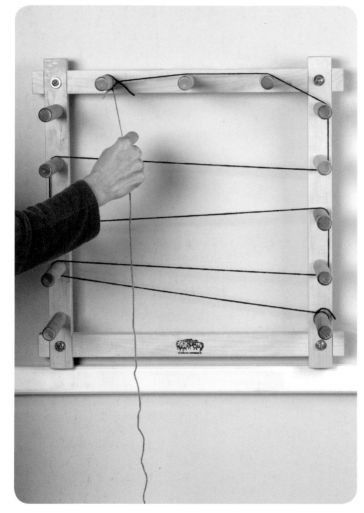

Tie one end of the warp to the leader yarn.

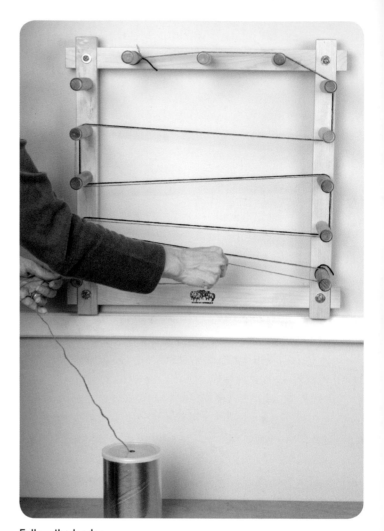

Follow the leader.

under tension. It's a good idea to choose a color that's different from the warp yarn. Measure 100" (254 cm) of the leader yarn, then add an extra 10" (25.5 cm) to allow for tying the ends of the leader onto the pegs of the warping board.

Tie the first 5" (12.5 cm) of the leader yarn to the upper left peg of the warping board. Bring the yarn across the top of the board to the upper right peg, then zig and zag it between pegs until you've used up all but the last 5" (12.5 cm), adjusting the path as necessary to end at a peg and taking

care not to cross the yarn on itself at any point. Tie the last 5" to the nearest peg. The leader yarn now shows the path to follow to measure 100" (254 cm) of yarn.

With the exception of forming the **cross**, winding the warp is now a simple matter of following the leader. The cross keeps the warp lengths in order, which is the key to minimizing tangles later. Place the warp yarn on the floor in front of the warping board. You can secure the yarn in a commercial cone or ball holder, or you can make your own. I like to use an empty coffee can

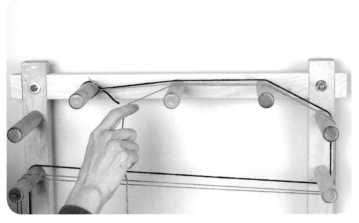

Form the cross on the first two pegs by always going over the second peg, under and over the first, then under the second.

or oatmeal box that has a well-fitting plastic lid. I cut a hole in the plastic lid, then place the cone or ball in the container, thread the yarn through the hole, and attach the lid. Then it's easy to wind the yarn without the yarn flopping around and getting tangled up on my legs.

Tie one end of the warping yarn to the top left peg of the warping board, in front of the leader yarn. Holding just enough tension to prevent the yarn from sagging, but not so much as to cause it to stretch, follow the path of the leader yarn exactly, ending *over* the peg where the end of the leader is tied. You have now wound one 100" (254 cm) length. To continue, wind the warp yarn around the bottom of the last peg, then follow the leader back to the second peg, placing the yarn next to (but not on top of) the yarn of the previous pass. Now it's time to form the all-important cross. Bring the yarn *over* the second peg, then *under* the first. You have now wound two 100" (254 cm) lengths. Next, bring the yarn and *over* the top of the first peg, then *under* the second, then follow the leader to the last peg for the third length. Continue in this manner, being careful to form the cross on the first two pegs by always going over the second peg, under the first, around the first, then under the second: over, under, over, under.

no warping board?

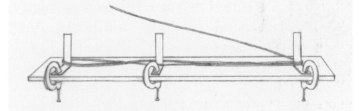

If you don't have a warping board, clamp two L-brackets about a foot away from each other on a stable surface. You will need enough room to extend the yarn to a third secured L-bracket 100" (254 cm) from the first bracket or the chosen length of your warp. You will form the cross between the first two brackets. This process usually involves locking the cat in another room and having someone watch the kids or other individuals who may be tempted to mess with your yarn.

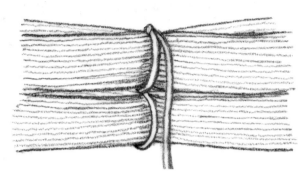

To keep track of the number of warp ends wound, loop a contrasting yarn around groups of 20 ends as you wind the warp.

As you wind the warp, be careful not to stretch the yarn or it will be shorter than you intended when released from the tension of the warping board. Also, with each pass of the warp yarn, take care to position the yarn on the pegs in front of the yarn from the previous pass so that the yarns are in parallel alignment. Otherwise, you'll create tangles that will give you grief later when you wind the warp onto the loom.

Each circular path of the warp represents two warp ends (you'll cut the loops at the first and last pegs later to separate them). To count warp ends, count the number of ends on top of the first or second peg and multiply this number by two. For our example, we want a total of 66 warp ends, so we should stop winding when there are 33 threads on the top of the first peg (or 66 threads on any other peg except the last one). To help you keep track of your progress, you may find it helpful to use a 20" (51 cm) length of contrasting yarn to wrap around every 20 warps as you go. When you have the correct number of ends, cut the warp yarn and tie the end to the first or last peg (depending on whether you want an even or odd number of ends), just like you tied the yarn when you began winding. If your project calls for a warp that fills the entire width of the reed, wind

Use a contrasting yarn to tie a choke tie on the warp at the same distance from the first peg as your loom measures from the back beam to the front beam.

To hold the cross, place your thumb on the right side of the cross, your index finger on top, your ring finger on the bottom, and your middle finger on the left side as you gently slide the cross off the pegs.

the warp in two smaller sections rather than one large one to make the next step easier.

Before you take the yarn off the warping board, measure the length on your loom from the back beam to the front beam. Measure the same distance from the first peg to mark placement of the **choke tie**. The choke tie is a 20" (51 cm) length of contrasting yarn tied around the entire bundle of warp yarns to keep them from slipping as you thread the rigid heddle. You can use the same yarn you used to count groups of 20 when you wound the warp. The choke will be used to tie the warp to the front beam after the threaded rigid heddle is placed in the loom. This allows you to tie the warp onto the back beam without the threads slipping and inadvertently shortening the warp length. You can also use choke ties on the four parts of the cross, but I find this overkill.

Transfer the Warp to the Loom

Before you continue, take a little break—visit the bathroom, have a cup of tea—then turn off your phone. Once you take the warp off the warping board, you don't want to be interrupted until it's completely threaded through the reed.

The most important thing to remember when removing the warp from the warping board is to maintain the integrity of the cross. Using your non-dominant hand (i.e., your left hand if you're right handed; your right hand if you're left handed), place your thumb on the right side of the cross, your index finger on top, your ring finger on the bottom, and your middle finger on the left side. This will secure the four parts of the cross as you remove it from the loom and transfer it to the rigid heddle. Gently slide the warp off the first and last pegs, draping the cross over your dominant hand.

Thread the first color in the appropriate holes and slots.

Thread the second color in the vacant holes and slots.

multiple warp colors

If you want more than one color in your warp, you can wind the warp in the desired color sequence, tying off the colors at the first or last peg at color changes, or you can wind each warp color separately. In general, it takes longer to change colors while you're winding, but the colors will be in the correct order when you thread the reed. I find it easiest to wind a separate warp for each color. When it's time to thread the warp through the reed, I thread one color, skipping holes and slots where I want the second color to be, then thread the second color in the vacant holes and slots.

Threading the Rigid Heddle

(*Note:* The photos in this section are shown on a Schacht loom.)

To hold the rigid heddle steady as you thread the warp ends through the holes and slots (i.e., the reed), place the rigid heddle in its working position on the loom (be sure to secure the rigid heddle so it doesn't accidentally fall out of the brackets) or secure it in a special stand—called a **reed stand**—designed for this purpose. A reed stand props the rigid heddle at a comfortable angle for threading. If you don't have a reed stand, you can fashion your own with two large spring-loaded clamps, two L-brackets, and one small clamp. Use the large clamps to secure the L-brackets to the top of a table, spaced apart an inch closer together than the reed width. Prop the rigid heddle against the backs of the brackets and secure it to the top of the L-bracket with the small clamp. Whether you use a commercial reed stand or one that you make yourself, it's helpful to place an extra clamp on the worktable adjacent to your dominant hand. You can use this clamp to wind the excess warp on while you're threading the reed so it doesn't get tangled or use it to store the cross if you must get up (see sidebar on page 33).

If you thread the reed while the rigid heddle is in position on the loom, it is helpful to tie the choke to the front beam before you start threading and wind the excess warp length around the clamp on the worktable. This will decrease tangling and keep the weight of the warp from the pulling the threads out of the rigid heddle.

To ensure that the warp is centered on the loom, place a tape measure at the center of the rigid heddle—I mark this spot with a permanent marker for easy reference. Measure half the distance of your desired weaving width in the direction of your dominant hand. For our example of a 6.6" (16.8 cm) warp, we'd mea-

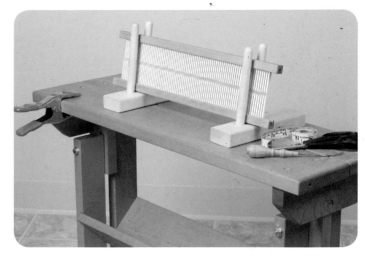

A reed stand holds the rigid heddle steady while it is threaded.

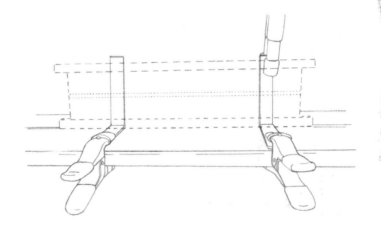

You can make your own reed stand with two large clamps, two L-brackets, and one small clamp.

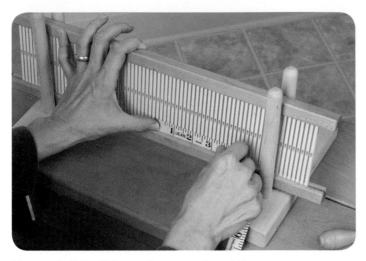

Measure half the distance of your weaving width.

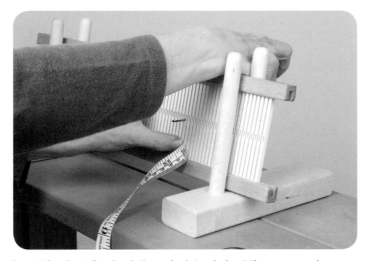

Insert the threading hook through slot or hole at the measured distance.

sure 3.3" (8.4 cm) from the center point. Because most tape measures are marked in eighths of inches instead of tenths, I use the tape to measure the inches, then I eyeball the fraction. Insert the threading hook through the slot or hole that corresponds to 3.3" (8.4 cm) from the center so that the handle of the hook is at the back of the reed and the hook is in front. This is where you'll thread the first warp end.

Wrap the length of the warp around clamp on the worktable.

With the cross secured in your non-dominant hand, use your other hand to cut the loops so that all of the threads hang free at this end of the warp bundle. Holding the cross in your hand with your palm facing up-wards, use your other hand to pick up the first warp thread and fold it into a loop, then grasp it between the thumb and index finger of the hand holding the cross. With your dominant hand, use the threading hook to grab the loop and pull it though the marked hole or slot of the reed. Make sure to pull at least two feet through the hole so that it won't slip. Fold the end of the next warp thread into a loop and use the hook to pull it through the next hole or slot toward the center of the reed. Continue in this manner, alternating holes and slots until all the warp ends have been threaded.

Cut the loops at the end of the cross.

Use the threading hook to pull loop through the first slot or hole.

Hold the cross with your palm up and use your other hand to thread the individual ends through the rigid heddle.

Form a loop with the first yarn length and hold it with the hand holding the cross.

in case of emergencies

If you absolutely must put down the warp before you're finished threading the holes and slots in the rigid heddle, be sure to secure the cross in some manner. For such emergencies, I have a steel spring-clamp attached to my worktable. It's large handles are a perfect place to store the cross so it remains intact until I can hold it again. Place the cross "upside down" between the two handles of the clamp. Allow the loose ends of the cross to dangle free from the lower handle and drape the length of warp on the worktable. Place a heavy object such as a book or another clamp (I have dozens of them around my work-space) on the warp to prevent it from slipping.

Use a steel clamp to secure the cross in an emergency.

Working towards the center of the rigid heddle, use the hook to pull the individual warp ends through adjacent slots and holes.

Winding On

The final step is to wind the yarn onto the loom and place it under tension. You'll want a pair of scissors handy, as well as smooth sturdy paper (cut up paper bags work well) or thin warp sticks (sold separately and cut to order) to place between the layers as the warp is wound around the back beam.

If you used a reed stand, carefully lift the rigid heddle out of the stand and place it in the neutral position in the heddle blocks, being sure to orientate it so that the choke tie is at the front of the loom and the cut ends are at the back of the loom. Use the loose ends of the choke to tie the warp to the front or cloth beam. Wrap the warp around the cloth beam a few times to keep it out of the way as you work. Bring the back apron rod over the top of the back beam and close to the threads coming out of the rigid heddle. Divide the warp in half and starting from the center, tie 1" (2.5 cm) bundles of the warp—you can eyeball this; it doesn't have to be exact—onto the back apron rod in secure square knots, striving to use the same amount of yarn in each knot. To make a square knot, divide the one-inch bundles in half and bring each half over the top of the apron rod and around the outside of the warp bundle (see page 36). Tie the two parts of a square knot on top of the warp to secure it to the apron rod.

With scissors, cut the choke tie so that the warp ends can spread out to the threaded width of the reed. Stand to the side of the loom and turn the crank with your dominant hand to wind the warp around the back beam, stopping before the warp forms a second layer on the beam. Slip the smooth sturdy paper or warping sticks between the warp layers to prevent the layers from interfering with one another (the paper will advance along with the warp as you turn the crank; if you're using warping sticks, add more sticks as necessary). As you wind the warp, resist the temptation to

Place the rigid heddle in the loom (shown on a loom stand here).

Tie the choke to the front or cloth beam.

"rake" the warp ends with your fingers. In fact, the less you touch the warp the better—the individual ends will straighten themselves out as they pass though the heddle and manipulating it with your fingers at this point may only cause tension problems later.

After you've wound a few turns, go to the front of the loom, grasp the warp firmly in one hand while using the other hand to steady the loom. Pull on the warp as a unit (do not pull individual threads) with firm and even tension to remove any slack in the wound warp.

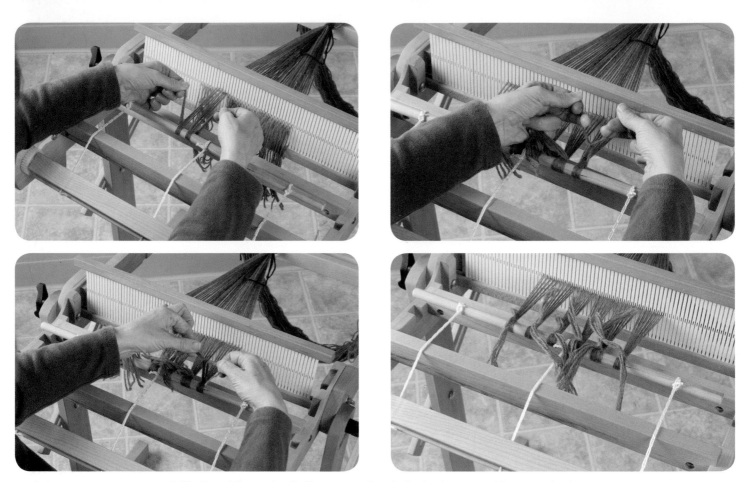

1. Starting at the center, tie the warp ends onto the back apron rod in square knots.

Tie 1" (2.5 cm) warp bundles around the apron rod in square knots.

2. Wind the warp around the back beam for one revolution, stopping before the warp winds on itself.

3. Slip the sturdy paper (or warping sticks) between the warp layers to keep them from interfering with one another.

4. Continue to advance the warp between layers of paper (or warping sticks).

5. After a few revolutions, pull on the unwound warp as a unit to remove slack in the wound warp.

Return to the side of the loom and wind a few more turns, adding sheets of paper as necessary to maintain a continuous boundary between warp layers, then move to the front of the loom and pull on the warp again. Continue to go back and forth between winding a few turns and pulling the yarn at the front to remove slack until about 12" (30.5 cm) of warp remains in front of the reed. The next (and final) step is to tie the warp to the front apron rod. But before you do, take a few min-utes to double check the threading in the reed. Make sure that you didn't miss any holes or slots in the reed and that there is just one warp thread in each (there will be times when you'll *want* skipped holes or slots or double threads, but this isn't one of them).

Now go to the front of the loom and pull the front apron rod over the front beam, close to the dangling warp ends. Use scissors to evenly cut the loops at the end of the warp so that the ends are completely separate from one another.

6. Cut the loops at the end of the warp to separate the ends.

7. Tie the ends in bundles to the front apron rod using the first half of square knots.

8. Pull on the tails of the knots to tighten the warp uniformly.

9. Pat the warp to check for loose or tight bundles. Adjust as necessary, then tie the second half of each square knot.

Divide the warp in half as you did when tying onto the back apron rod, and working from the center out to the sides, tie the warp onto the front apron rod in 1" (2.5 cm) bundles, tying just the first half of a square knot for each bundle. Beginning at the center and working one group at a time outward to the edges, pull on the tails of the first half-knot to tighten the slack in the warp. When the tension feels even, tie the second half of the knot to secure the warp, striving to produce the same amount of tension on each group. To check that the tension is even, pat the warp threads gently with your hand. If you feel any soft spots, correct the tension by tightening up the corresponding knots.

Next, put the rigid heddle in the up position in the heddle blocks to make sure that every other thread is lifted. There will be a significant space between the lifted threads (those threaded through the holes) and the stationary threads (those threaded in the slots). This is the **shed**. Now put the rigid heddle in the down position and notice that every other thread is now lowered. By moving the rigid heddle up and down, you'll create two different sheds through which to place the weft yarn. That's all there is to it; well, almost. Read on.

WEAVING

To weave cloth, the weft must travel across the warp threads in an over-under-over pattern. To facilitate this, the rigid heddle is alternately lifted and lowered to lift and lower alternate warp ends (the ones that were threaded through the holes in the rigid heddle) while the weft is passed back and forth across the warp. The rigid heddle is used to straighten and align each pass of the weft. Weaving is a simple manner of lifting half the warp, passing the shuttle through the shed, positioning it with the rigid heddle, lowering half the warp, passing the shuttle through the shed in the opposite direction, positioning it, then repeating the process, over and over.

When the weft travels over and under adjacent warp ends, **plain weave** cloth is woven.

Winding the Shuttle

Shuttles are used to hold the weft yarn in an orderly manner to facilitate the weaving process. Shuttles come in all shapes and sizes designed to help with various weaving techniques. The most popular shuttle for rigid heddle looms is a stick shuttle.

You'll want to wind as much weft as possible on the shuttle without inhibiting its ability to pass easily through the shed. Start by winding several rotations along the middle of the shuttle, then several figure eights along each side. Repeat several passes of each of these motions until the shuttle is comfortably full of weft yarn.

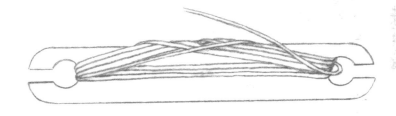

Wind warp on a stick shuttle along the center and in figure eights on each edge (shown on one edge only here).

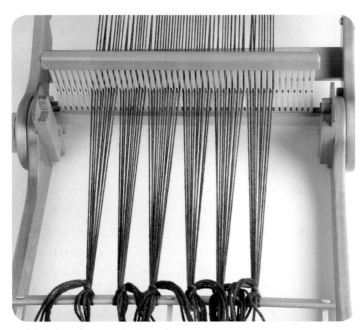

The warp will bunch together where it's tied to the apron rod.

Weave an inch or two with waste yarn to bring the warp to its full width.

Weaving at Last

Notice how the warp bunches together at each group that's tied to the apron rod. The "real" cloth doesn't begin until these spaces are uniform and the warp is at its full width. It usually takes about an inch or two of weaving, called the **header**, to bring the warp to its full width. Therefore, you may want to weave this initial part with waste yarn (you'll remove it before finishing the cloth). The length of the warp between the beginning of the full-width cloth and the knots on the apron rod can be used as fringe—more on that later.

Each pass of the shuttle is called a **shot**. After each shot, the rigid heddle is pulled toward the front beam to align the weft perpendicular to the warp and "beat" it close to the previous weft shot. Because of this action, the rigid heddle is also referred to as the **beater**. The leading edge of the woven cloth, where the next shot of weft will be placed, is called the **fell**. The fell line is perpendicular to the warp threads. Once the weft is woven, each woven thread is referred to as a **pick.**

To begin, put the rigid heddle in the up position. Unwind enough yarn from the shuttle to extend about 3" (7.5 cm) beyond the width of the warp. Then pass the shuttle through the shed so that a tail of weft about 3" (7.5 cm) long hangs free beyond the selvedge. Pull the rigid heddle forward to align the weft perpendicular to the warp. You have now woven one pick. Place the rigid heddle in the down position. Tuck the free weft tail about 2" (5 cm) into the shed and allow it to exit out of the shed (you'll trim it later). Then unwind a bit more yarn from the shuttle and pass the shuttle through the shed in the opposite direction, placing the weft at a 45-degree angle. Pull the rigid heddle forward to align this pick with the previous one. It is important to maintain a 45-degree angle when laying the weft yarn in place. This angle will provide necessary extra length for the weft to travel over and under the individual warp threads.

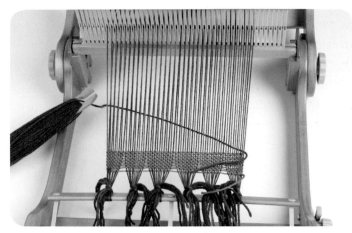

Pass the shuttle through the first shed, leaving a 3" (7.5 cm) tail at the selvedge edge.

Change sheds and tuck the weft tail into the new shed for about 2" (5 cm).

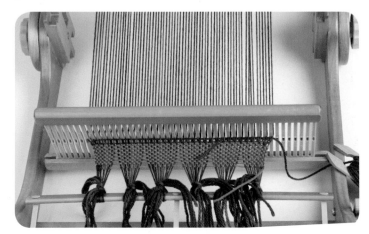

Pull the rigid heddle forward to align the weft picks.

Continue weaving by moving the heddle up or down, placing yarn in the shed, and beating it into place. Each pick will reduce the size of the shed, and it won't be long before the shed is too small to allow the shuttle to be passed through at a 45-degree angle. At this point, you'll need to **advance the warp**. To advance the warp, release the tension from the front and back beams by pulling forward on the levers that release the front and back brakes, then wind the woven cloth onto the front beam to make more space for the shed, being sure to stop winding when the fell line is still in front of the front beam. It's a good idea to place smooth paper between the first few revolutions of the cloth on the front beam, just as you did when winding the warp on the back beam. This will allow the cloth to wind onto the front beam evenly and decrease tension problems in the warp later. In most cases, it is not necessary to place paper between each layer, just the first few times around.

Mind Your Selvedges

One of the hallmarks of beautiful cloth is straight edges or **selvedges**. Although the weft appears to follow a straight line from selvedge edge to selvedge edge, it actually follows a sinuous path as it bends over and under the individual warp threads. To allow for the extra length needed for this sinuous path, pass the shuttle through the shed at an angle to the warp. For balanced weaves, 45 degrees is about right; for warp-faced weaves (in which there are fewer warp ends to travel over and under), 20 degrees is about right. You'll want to experiment to determine what's best for each project (this is one reason why it's a good idea to allow for sampling when measuring the warp). If the angle is too small, the selvedges will draw in toward the center and crowd the warp threads; if it's too large, loops may form at the selvedges. Even experienced weavers can have trouble getting straight selvedges, so don't despair if yours aren't

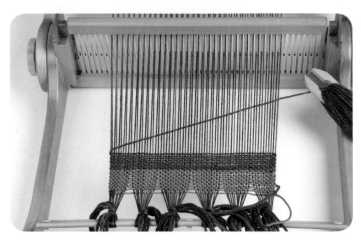

Place the weft in the shed at a 45-degree angle to provide enough slack for a balanced weave.

If there isn't enough slack in the weft, the selvedges will draw in.

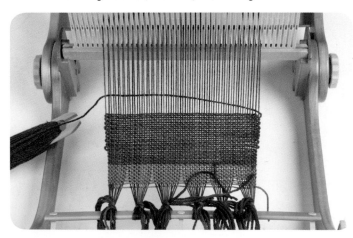

If there is too much slack in the weft, loops may form at the selvedges.

perfect. Like all acquired skills, it takes practice. Don't get too concerned about doing anything exactly "right;" as long as you do anything consistently, it will appear intentional!

Find Your Beat

Another key to beautiful cloth is consistent spaces between individual weft picks. The spacing between the warp ends is made uniform when the warp is threaded through the reed. Once a loom is warped, you don't have to worry about them. But the spacing between individual weft picks depends on how firmly you beat each pick with the rigid heddle, and that can vary a lot. Consider the photo below. The first inch was woven with a firm beat that packed the weft picks close to one another. In this section, there are more weft picks per inch than warp ends. The second inch was woven with a light beat that allowed considerable space between individual picks. In this section, there are fewer weft picks per inch than warp ends. The third inch was woven with an intermediate beat that produced the same number of weft picks per inch as warp ends. This section is woven with a balanced beat.

Depending on the look you want for your cloth, you may choose a firm, light, or balanced beat. All are fine.

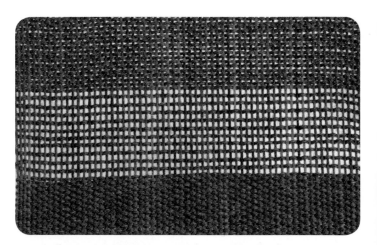

From bottom to top, this warp was woven with a firm beat, a light beat, and a balanced beat.

But whichever you choose, you want to be consistent throughout the entire project. You may find it helpful to periodically unwind the cloth from the front beam to check that you've maintained a consistent beat (i.e., the weft picks are evenly spaced). This isn't as hard as it sounds—you'll quickly settle into a rhythm of forming the shed, passing the shuttle, and beating the weft, and this rhythm will result in uniform cloth. It's this rhythm that draws people to weaving.

Join New Weft

If you run out of yarn on your shuttle or the weft breaks, there is a simple method to start a yarn. Open a new shed and place the tail of the old yarn into the new shed at an angle, allowing it to exit on top of the warp. Bring the new yarn into the shed until it overlaps the old yarn, then exit its tail a few inches from the exiting tail of the old yarn and beat. Continue weaving and trim the tails after you have woven a few picks.

measuring your progress

Once the cloth is rolled on the front beam it can be hard to tell how much cloth you have woven. A simple way to keep track is to measure the cloth as you weave. Before the cloth begins to wind on the front beam, use a tape measure to measure the amount that you've woven (be sure to begin your measurement where the warp is spread to its full width). Mark one selvedge with a contrasting thread and make a note of this measurement. Continue to weave until this marker thread reaches the front beam, then mark the selvedge with another contrasting thread. Add up the distances between marker threads to measure your progress.

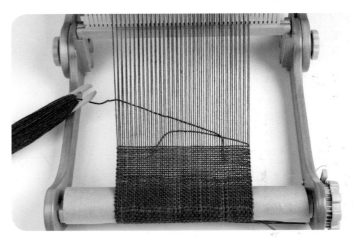

To join new weft yarn, overlap the old and new yarns for about 2" (5 cm), allowing tails of each to exit the warp.

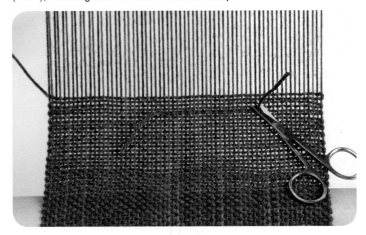

After you've woven a few picks, trim the ends.

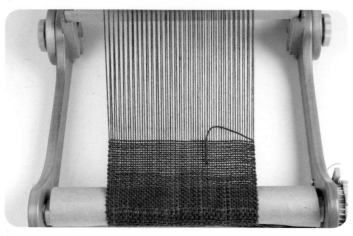

Place the end of the old weft at an angle in the next shed, leaving a tail on top.

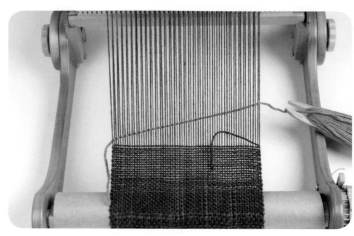

Bring the new yarn into the shed from the other side, leaving a tail at the selvedge.

Tuck the weft tail in the same shed as the second pick and beat them together.

Add New Color

To add a new color, start by cutting the yarn you have been working leaving a generous tail. Open a new shed and place the tail back into the shed bringing it up above the warp a couple of inches from the selvedge, leaving it at an angle. Starting from the opposite side of where you ended the old color, place the new color in the same shed, also at an angle and leaving a tail of this color hanging out from the edge.

Beat the yarns, then change the shed. Bring the new color tail back into the weft at an angle. Lay in a second pick of the new color, then beat it into place. Continue weaving as usual with the new yarn. After you've woven an inch or two, trim the tails close to the surface of the cloth.

weaving with two shuttles

1. Place the first shuttle within easy reach as you weave with the second.

2. Place the second shuttle next to the first.

3. Pick up first shuttle from under the second. Continue to weave, always picking up the new color from under the old.

4. After you've woven a few inches, trim the tails.

Weaving with two shuttles isn't any more difficult than weaving with one, but it is important that you're consistent with how you manipulate the two at the selvedges. For example, let's say you wanted to weave narrow two-pick stripes of red and brown for the Grab It and Go Bag on page 84. You'd begin by winding each color on a separate shuttle. Weave two picks of red in the usual manner, then place the shuttle within easy reach beside you, in your lap, or on the loom. Beginning from the same side that the red started, weave two picks with brown and place that shuttle within easy reach. Pick up the red shuttle so that the red yarn comes from under the brown, then weave two picks with red. Continue in this manner, always picking up new color from under the old. You may find that the selvedges aren't perfectly straight, but as long as you are consistent in how the yarns cross at the edges, you'll create a decorative repeating pattern on the selvedges. After weaving a few inches, trim the beginning tails.

Use these principles even if the pattern isn't worked in twos. You may have to experiment with which side you enter the first versus second color, just be sure to always go under the previously worked thread.

THE END'S IN SIGHT

To finish, work a few picks with scrap yarn to hold the last picks of the cloth in place. Untie the warp from the front and back beams and pull the cloth off of the loom. If you don't plan to use any of the loom waste for fringe (or if you're sure to leave enough length for fringe before you cut), you can cut the warp near the apron rods instead of untying them, then untie the knots and throw them away. These waste yarns are called **thrums**. Some weavers save them obsessively and tie them together to use a weft for another project. They can also be used for pom-poms or fringe.

Finishing Techniques

You have a few choices for finishing your weaving. Most of the projects in this book are finished with knotted or twisted fringe or with hemstitching, followed by fulling or gentle washing.

Hemstitching is worked with a needle and weft yarn while the project is still on the loom (see page 120). It holds the weft in place and creates a tidy edge for fringe. To finish, simply remove the scrap yarn from the header after stitching (scrap yarn is not necessary at the final edge of cloth that has been hemstitched).

If you want a knotted or twisted **fringe**, trim the warp ends a few inches longer than the desired fringe length to keep the ends manageable. Place the cloth near the edge of a table so that a short end hangs off the edge. Place a book or other weight on top of the cloth to prevent it from slipping. Sit on a short stool or the floor so that the working ends are at eye level. Remove the scrap yarn at the end of the cloth and knot or twist the fringe as desired (see page 121). Repeat for the other end of the cloth.

If you want to create a dense, sturdy cloth, **full** it by subjecting it to water, soap, and agitation (see page 55).

Fulling isn't an exact science so it's important to monitor the progress. Because fulling involves shrinkage of the fibers, there's no going back to "unfull" an "over-fulled" cloth.

Most handwovens should be washed by hand. To do this, fill a basin or tub with lukewarm water and add about a teaspoon of delicate soap. Gently agitate the cloth with your hands, being careful not to agitate so much that fulling occurs. Remove the cloth from the water, drain the water, refill the basin with clean water, and return the cloth to rinse it. Repeat the rinse process as many times as necessary to remove all the soap from the cloth. Gently squeeze out the water, then roll the cloth in a clean towel to remove excess moisture. Lay it flat to dry.

Once the cloth is dry, use scissors or a rotary cutter against a self-healing mat to trim the fringe straight and to the desired length.

PROBLEM SOLVING

The most important thing to know about weaving mistakes is that none is insurmountable. I have lost my cross, wound short warps, hacked color order, and had more tension problems than a Wall Street broker on a bad day. I have, however, never lost the battle. Sometimes it takes me longer to do a task than I thought it would, but everything is fixable (or the fabric turns into something other than originally envisioned). The most important lesson I've learned is that if things are going wrong, it's sometimes best to walk away. A good night's sleep can completely change my perspective. The second most important thing I've learned is that it is better to fix small mistakes as soon as they crop up so they don't become big problems later. The three problems you're most likely to encounter are broken warp threads, weft floats or skips, and tension problems.

Broken Warp Threads

A broken warp end doesn't ruin a project. If a warp end breaks, simply pull that end free from the rigid heddle and replace it with a new piece of yarn. You'll need a T-pin and a small weight (I like to use plastic film canisters—which are becoming scarce—filled with dried beans or beads). To start, place the T-pin into the woven cloth a few picks away from the fell line and so that the head is even with the gap left by the broken warp thread. Cut a new piece of warp about

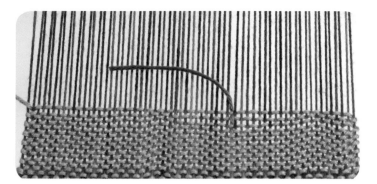

1. Pull the broken warp end to the front of the loom.

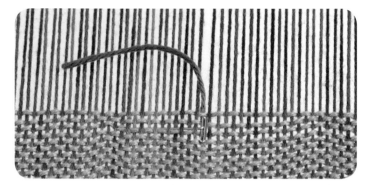

2. Tuck a T-pin into the woven cloth so that the head is even with the gap left by the broken warp thread.

3. Wrap one end of the new warp around the head of a T-pin.

4. Secure the new warp in a weighted canister or jar and let it hang off the back of the loom.

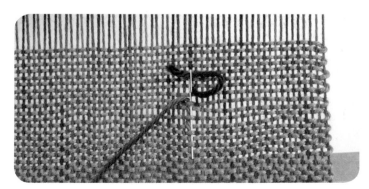

5. After weaving an inch of cloth, needle weave the new warp tail down the cloth.

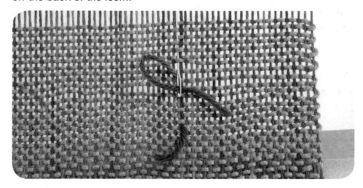

6. Needle weave the old warp tail up the cloth.

Floats occur when the weft doesn't travel over and under the warp properly.

To fix a float, thread a piece of weft yarn on a tapestry needle and needle weave the yarn along the correct path.

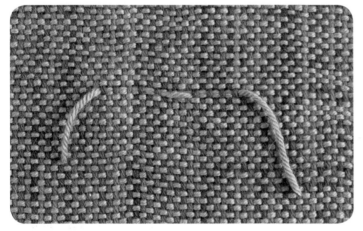

After washing the fabric, trim the ends of the replacement weft and cut the original weft at each end of the float.

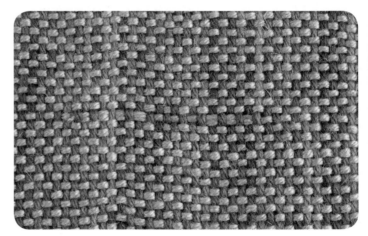

The correction is barely visible in the finished cloth.

18" (45.5 cm) longer than the length of the warp you think you have left to weave. Wrap one end of the new warp around the head of the T-pin. Thread the other end of the new warp through the vacant slot or hole in the rigid heddle to the back of the loom. Roll the end of the warp into a ball, place the ball in the container, and secure the lid so that the container hangs over the back beam and dangles in the air. Continue weaving as usual for a few inches to secure the new warp. Remove the T-pin and needle weave (see page 120) the old and new warp ends into the fabric. Trim the tails.

Weft Floats

Once the cloth is off the loom, take a good look at each side of the cloth to check for warp or weft skips or **floats**. Floats occur when a weft pick doesn't travel over and under the warp ends properly. They are generally caused when adjacent warp threads stick together so that a thread that was supposed to be raised doesn't go up or a thread that was supposed to be lowered doesn't go down. Get in the habit of checking for "clean" sheds to ensure against this and pay attention to the cloth as you weave. It's much easier to "unweave" a few picks to correct a float than to fix it after the cloth is off the loom.

If you do find a float after the cloth is off the loom, you can fix it with a bit of weft yarn threaded on a tapestry needle. Beginning and ending about an inch from the float, needle weave the yarn along the correct path. Wash the fabric to set the yarn. Trim the tails of the new weft, then cut the old weft at the float and trim those tails.

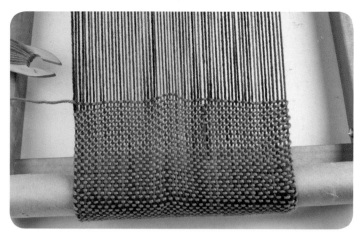

The weft will follow a wavy path if the warp is under uneven tension.

Tension Problems

Hopefully you can catch tension problems right away and fix them before they become a nuisance. If you've tied the warp to the apron rods with uneven tension across the width of the warp, the first few weft picks will appear wavy. To fix this problem, simply unweave the first few picks and retie the warp with even tension.

Sometimes the problem is that the warp wasn't wound evenly on the back beam, which causes individual warp ends to loosen. To tighten these ends (or groups of ends), cut a piece of scrap yarn about 12" (30.5 cm) long, loop it around the loose thread(s) at the back beam, and secure the tails of the waste yarn in a weighted canister as used for fixing broken warp ends.

getting up to warp speed

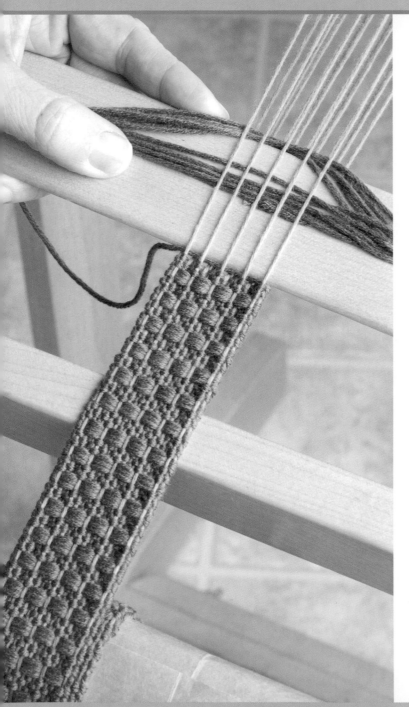

When most people think of weaving, they think of the part where the shuttle is passed back and forth and the weft is beat into place—which is, in fact, called "weaving." Most tend to forget that planning, warping, and finishing are also important parts of the process. Here is a way to approach the process in small steps so you don't feel like all the preparation just gets in the way of weaving.

Sunday

Plan your project. To start, take a mug of your favorite beverage to a quiet sunny spot. Surround yourselves with yarns, calculator, project planning sheet, colored pencils and paper, and inspiring books, photos, or samples of cloth. If you plan to work from a pattern, check to make sure you have everything you need. If not, you might need to make a trip to the yarn store (gosh, darn). If you plan to design your own project or modify an existing one, start with a vision of what you want, then plan how you'll achieve it. Choose the yarn and calculate the warp and weft amounts (use the project planning sheet on page 124). Feel free to doodle, sketch, and imagine all aspects of your project from start to finish. This is the dreamy stage when all things are possible—relish it!

Note: The tasks for Monday, Tuesday, and Wednesday usually average around twenty minutes apiece. You may want to have the Warping Checklist on page 123 handy as you work. If you feel energetic, feel free to do all three on the same day and get weaving even faster!

Monday

Measure the warp. You've already spent time readjusting to the work week—answering e-mails, making phone calls, attending meetings, and whatever else is involved in your week-day routine—and you probably don't have much extra energy. Grab your project notes, measure off the leader string, wind the warp, and tie your choke. Then walk away. That's all you have to do today!

Tuesday

Thread the heddles. Take a big breath of fresh air and plop yourself down in front of the reed and start threading. You'll want to have clear focus when you do this so pick the time of day that's best for you. Take advice from your third-grade math teacher and check your work!

Wednesday

Wind the warp onto the loom. It's hump day and time for an energizing task. For me, this is when it all comes together. As I watch those threads glide onto the loom, I envision all the possibilities ahead. I usually make plans for a bit of sampling (but, wait, I'm getting ahead of myself).

Thursday

Sample. Thursdays are the new Fridays. It's time to gear up for the upcoming weekend. Celebrate by doing some sample weaving. Use that extra ten inches of warp to tinker with colors you might not ordinarily use, practice a bit of lace, or simply weave a few inches of your project to get a handle on how firmly you want to beat the weft.

Friday

It's the weekend and time to weave! This is usually the day I stay up late and listen to a book on tape or watch a movie with my family while getting a good start on my project. I sometimes get together with friends to work on projects together.

Saturday

Keep up the good work. Set aside part of the morning, afternoon, or evening to finish up your project. Depending on how ambitious you were, you can probably finish in a few delicious hours between errands, exercise, family time, and other weekend chores.

Sunday

(I know that this is technically a week and a day, but since I usually start planning for my next project while finishing the last, I don't count it!) As you are gearing back up for work, settle in for a bit of finishing time. If you hemstitched your ends, this could just mean washing, or you can try a new elaborate fringe. Now you can sit back and admire your handiwork. Job well done.

A Final Note: If at anytime in the process you feel discouraged or if things aren't working the way you like—walk away! Some days it seems that nothing goes right. Give yourself a little time, then come back to it fresh—you'll have renewed energy to tackle any problem, especially when approached in small tasks at a time.

WARPING

Warp the loom (see page 24), following the specifications on page 53.

WEAVING

Weave a few inches of header to spread the warp ends (see page 40).

Weave with the forest green for at least 5" (12.5 cm) for a sample (you may try other colors of wool of the same brand) to test shrinkage later. Wools tend to shrink differently, and you will use this sample to test the amount of washing it will take to get the degree of fulling that you want—once the cloth is fulled there is no going back! Leave 3" (7.5 cm) of unwoven warp between the end of the sample and the beginning of the scarf. Weave 90" (229 cm) with forest green.

FINISHING

Remove the fabric from the loom (see page 46) by untying the warp from the apron rods. Remove the scrap yarn in the header. With sharp scissors, cut the sample section from the scarf.

Fulling

Full (see box at right) the sample to the desired thickness, then full the scarf to match (expect about 30% to be lost in width and length). Allow the fabric to thoroughly air-dry. Trim the loose threads from each end of the scarf.

Fringe

Using sharp scissors, cut fifteen slits at each end of the scarf, each about 2" (5 cm) long and about ¼" (6 mm) apart to form fringe.

the full story

The terms "fulling" and "felting" are often used interchangeably, although they refer to slightly different techniques. Felting is the process of agitating unspun protein fibers, such as wool, with needles or water to fuse the fibers together into a solid fabric. Fulling is the same process as felting—permanently interlocking microscopic barbs on protein fibers with agitation—but it is applied to wool yarn that has already been woven, knitted, or crocheted.

Fulling typically results in a fabric with more drape while felting produces a sturdier, denser fabric. However, heavily fulled cloth can become very dense and felt-like, often resulting in fabric that can be cut without fraying. Either one causes the fabric to shrink both in width and length. The amount of shrinkage will vary with the yarn, water temperature, and amount of agitation.

Try combining yarns that full (wool and alpaca, for example) with yarns that don't (cotton, linen, rayon, and synthetics, for example). Called "differential shrinkage," this can cause wonderful bumps and textures in woven fabric.

Fulling Woven Fabric

It's easiest to full fabric in a top-loading washing machine (front-loading machines have no agitator to encourage fulling, and it's impossible to open the machine mid-cycle to check on progress without flooding the laundry room). Because all washing machines are a little different, you'll want to use a sample to test the amount of shrinkage before you full your entire project. Measure your sample before and after it goes through the washing machine to determine how much length and width will be lost by fulling.

For a lightly fulled fabric, set the machine on the delicate cycle (which has limited agitation) and warm water on a low water level. Let the machine fill with water, then add a couple of teaspoons of delicate washing soap along with the sample. Let the agitator run for a minute, then check the cloth to see how much fulling has occurred. If you're satisfied with the degree of fulling, remove the fabric from the machine, otherwise let it continue to agitate, checking the progress every minute or so. If the desired amount of fulling occurs before the rinse cycle begins, gently hand-rinse the fabric to remove the soap without causing further felting. Roll the sample in a towel to remove excess moisture, then lay it flat.

Decide if your sample fulled more or less than you want in the finished project. If you want your project to be less fulled, remove it from the washing machine sooner. If you want it more fulled, repeat the process exactly.

For a heavily fulled fabric, set the machine on the regular cycle, which has substantial agitation, but check the progress every few minutes to make sure that the fabric doesn't get too dense. While it's possible to repeat the process to make the fabric denser, there's no going back to undo fulling that has already occurred.

You can also full your fabric by hand. Simply fill a basin (or your bathtub if your project is large) with lukewarm water. Add soap and the fabric, then agitate the project vigorously with your hands until you have the level of fullness you desire. This can take anywhere from a few minutes to upward of an hour! Rinse the fabric to rid it of any soap, then roll it in a towel to remove water, and lay it flat to air-dry.

WARPING

Warp the loom (see page 24), following the specifications on page 57.

WEAVING

Weave a few inches of header to spread the warp ends (see page 40).

Weave 7" (18 cm) for each coaster, using a different weft color for each coaster.

FINISHING

Remove the fabric from the loom (see page 46). Remove the scrap yarn in the header.

Fulling

Full (see page 55) the entire length of coaster fabric in a single piece, using a lot of agitation to create a dense fabric that can be cut without fraying. Lay the fabric flat to air-dry thoroughly. With sharp scissors, cut the coasters apart at the color changes, then trim them to 4" (10 cm) squares.

Needlefelting

Embellish each coaster with free-form needlefelted flowers, following the instructions at right, beginning with the petal outline, then the petal center, and ending with the flower center.

needlefelting basics

Needlefelting is a nice way to embellish woven fabric. In order for the fiber to adhere to the fabric, both the fiber and fabric need to have a high content of wool. Depending on the look you want, you can needlefelt with yarn or coarse combed top or carded roving. Needlefelting involves jabbing the yarn or wool with a barbed wire that causes the fibers to interlock with one another. The wires, which come in various sizes, are available at weaving and craft shops. Use smaller needles for smaller designs, larger needles for larger ones. Be aware that these needles are very sharp. Take care not to stab your fingers and, because they can draw blood, never share your needles!

Lay the fabric to be embellished face up on top of a piece of thick foam rubber. The foam provides a safe surface for stabbing into and because foam is a synthetic, it won't interfere with the felting process.

Pull out a length or clump of roving about equal to the length of an individual fiber (about 3" [7.5 cm]). You'll want the ends to feather so pull the fibers apart instead of cutting them with scissors. To blend two or more colors, lay a small clump of each color on top of one another and use your fingers to gently loosen and blend them.

Arrange a thin layer of the fiber in the desired design on top of the fulled fabric. Use the felting needle to jab the fiber repeatedly in a straight up-and-down motion to fuse the fiber with the fabric. The more you jab, the more tightly the fiber will adhere (or felt) to the fabric. Jab enough so that the fibers can't be pulled off the fabric surface. Add thin layers as desired to create a smooth surface and the desired density of coverage. To obscure the ends of each layer of fiber, taper the ends by working along the feathered edges. Gently pull on the fibers to ensure that they are secure.

Depending on the density of the fabric, some of the felted fibers may push through to the wrong side of the fabric. You can trim them, but unless the foundation fabric is very thick and dense, they may be visible to some degree.

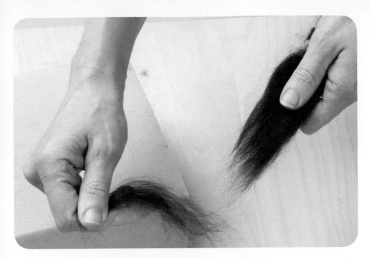

1. Pull out a length of fiber about 3" (7.5 cm) long.

2. To blend two or more colors, hold the colors together and pull on both to loosen the fibers.

3. Arrange the loosened fibers on the fulled cloth and use a felting needle to jab the fibers into cloth.

4. Add layers and colors as desired.

bobbled slippers

shrinking fabric on purpose provides endless opportunities for making shaped garments, bags, belts, and even shoes! If you combine yarns that shrink with yarns that don't in the warp and weft, your fabric will be covered in bumps. If you combine these yarns in the warp and use only a yarn that shrinks in the weft, you'll produce a fabric with long wavy stripes. Experiment to see what other effects you can produce.

Finished Dimensions
About 10" (25.5 cm) long; to fit a woman's foot.

Weave Structure
Plain weave with differential shrinkage.

Equipment
10-dent rigid heddle with 14" (35.5 cm) weaving width; two stick shuttles.

Warp and Weft Specifications

Sett (epi)
10.

Weaving Width
14" (35.5 cm).

Picks per Inch (ppi)
8.

Warp Length
100" (254 cm; includes 30" [76 cm] for loom waste and take-up).

Number of Warp Ends
141 doubled ends.

Warp and Weft Color Order
Warp: Using two threads together as one, alternate 3 yellow and 3 blue green, ending with 3 yellow.
Weft: Using two threads together as one, alternate 3 yellow and 3 mint green, ending with 3 yellow.

Yarns

Warp
2-ply 2/8 fingering-weight wool (2,240 yd [2,048 m]/lb): 400 yd (366 m) yellow.
2-ply 10/2 laceweight mercerized cotton (4,000 yd [3,352 m]/lb): 385 yd (352 m) blue-green.
Shown here: Jaggerspun Main Line 2/8 (100% wool) in Daffodil (yellow).
Lunatic Fringe 10/2 mercerized cotton (100% cotton) in Blue Green.

Weft
2-ply 2/8 fingering-weight wool (2,240 yd [2,048 m]/lb): 240 yd (219 m) yellow.
2-ply laceweight mercerized cotton (4,000 yd [3,352 m] lb): 239 yd (218.5 m) mint green.
Shown here: Jaggerspun Main Line 2/8 (100% wool) in Daffodil (yellow).
UKI 10/2 mercerized cotton (100% cotton) in Willow Green (mint green).

Trim
2-ply 3/8 sportweight wool (1,490 yd [1,362.5 m]/lb): 5 yd [4.5 m] green.
Shown here: Jaggerspun Main Line 3/8 (100% wool) in Capri Green.

WARPING

Measure the Warp

Because the warp is wound in pairs, it will help to use yarn wound on mini cones. Place two cones of yellow in a cone holder or in two tall, narrow containers. Wind the warp (see page 35) using two strands as one, placing a finger between the two to keep them from tangling. Wind 72 double-stranded ends. Tie a choke.

Place two blue-green cones in the holder or containers and wind 69 doubled-stranded ends of blue-green in the same manner. Tie a choke.

Wind the Shuttle

Place two cones of yellow in a cone holder or container and wind a shuttle (see page 39) with double strands of yellow. Wind another shuttle with double strands of mint green.

Thread the Reed

Warp the loom (see page 24), following the specifications on page 61, threading *3 yellow double-ends, then skipping 3 spaces; repeat from * for the entire 14" (35.5 cm) width. Thread the blue-green double-ends in the empty spaces. Check your work—it is easier to correct threading errors before the warp is wound onto the back beam.

WEAVING

Weave a few picks of cotton scrap yarn (cotton will be easy to remove) to spread the warp ends (see page 40). Using a loose beat, weave three picks with yellow. Add green and weave three picks with green. Alternate three picks each of yellow and green for the entire length of the warp (see page 45 for tips on working with two shuttles). Don't worry too much about maintaining even selvedges—they won't be seen in the final project.

FINISHING

Remove the fabric from the loom (see page 46). Remove the scrap yarn in the header.

Fulling

Full (see page 55) the entire length of the fabric in the washing machine set for a normal cycle with enough warm water to allow complete submersion. Check the fabric periodically for progress—you want it to shrink to about 5½" (14 cm) wide or until "bobbles" begin to appear. Reset the washer if necessary to get the desired amount of shrinkage. Remove the fabric from the washer and rinse it thoroughly, then roll it in a towel to squeeze out the excess moisture and lay it flat to air-dry.

Assembly

Photocopy the pattern pieces at right on stiff card stock, enlarging as necessary so that each square eguals 1" (2.4 cm). Cut the pieces out and pin them to the fabric. Cut the dry fabric, using the templates as a guide. Using yellow and an overhand stitch, sew one top flap to one sole, with the arch facing to the left, then sew the other top flap to the other sole, with the arch pointing to the right. Sew one back piece to each sole and front flap. Fold the extra fabric from the back piece so that it is even with the front flap and stay-stitch it in place by taking one stitch on each side. Using the green sportweight wool, sew decorative blanket stitches around the sole of each slipper.

Gently handwash the slippers in warm water using mild soap and rubbing the stitching to full it ever so slightly. Roll the slippers in a towel, then shape as desired (place a small cloth or tissue paper in the toes) and allow to air-dry completely.

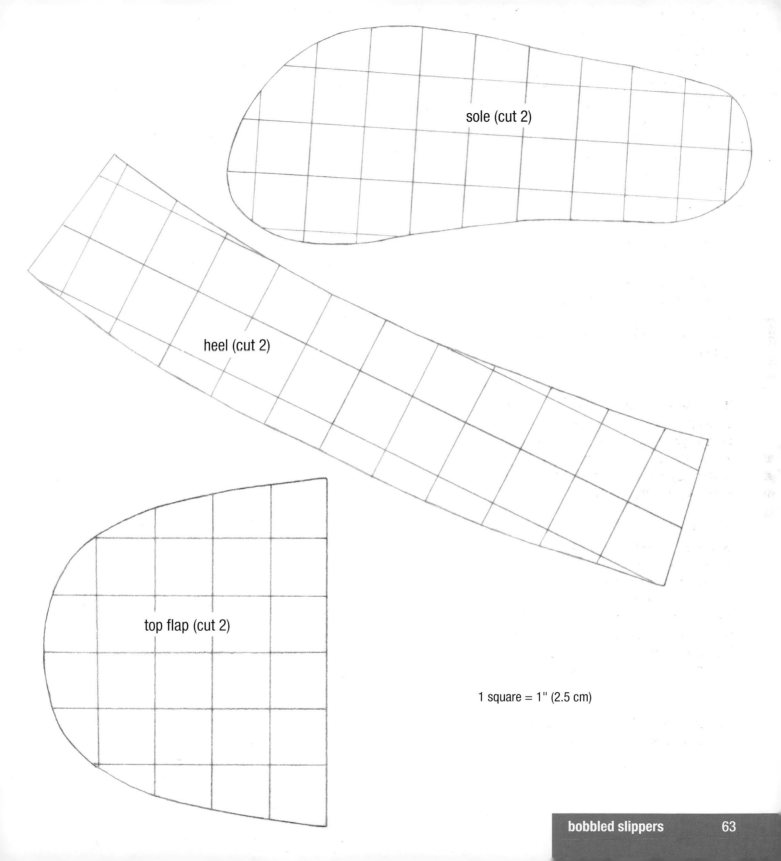

sole (cut 2)

heel (cut 2)

top flap (cut 2)

1 square = 1" (2.5 cm)

color-play **plaid**

plaid provides endless opportunities to play with color. This scarf uses two purples close in hue to provide subtle color play that stands in contrast to an analogous blue with a brighter value. Now if this sentence sounds like gobbledegook, it's because the terms "value," "hue," and "analogous" are words we used to describe color (see Color in Weaving, page 19). Said another way: Pick two similar purples and add a bright blue and see what happens! This scarf uses another nifty trick—a whipstitch is worked along each selvedge edge as the cloth is woven to visually balance the colors while masking potentially messy selvedges.

Finished Dimensions
About 8¼" (21 cm) wide by 53½" (136 cm) long, plus 2" (5 cm) fringe at each end.

Weave Structure
Balanced plain weave.

Equipment
10-dent rigid heddle with 9" (23 cm) weaving width; three stick shuttles; tapestry needle.

Warp and Weft Specifications
Sett (epi)
10.
Weaving Width
9" (23 cm).

Picks per Inch (ppi)
6.

Warp Length
100" (256 cm; includes 30" [76 cm] for yarn waste and take-up, and 10" [25.5 cm] for sampling).

Number of Warp Ends
90.

Warp Color Order
10 dark purple; 10 light purple; 10 ice blue; 10 light purple; 10 dark purple; 10 light purple; 10 ice blue; 10 light purple; 10 dark purple.

Weft Color Order
8 dark purple [6 light purple; 6 ice blue; 6 light purple; 6 dark purple] 15 times, end 8 dark purple.

Yarns

Warp
Bulky singles in a wool/mohair/cashmere blend (1,097 yd [1,003 m]/lb): 85 yd (77.5 m) dark purple, 115 yd (105 m) light purple, and 60 yd (55 m) ice blue.
Shown here: Harrisville Designs Orchid Yarns (70% fine wool, 25% mohair, 5% cashmere; 184 yd [168 m]/100 g): #255 Amethyst (dark purple), #256 Wisteria (light purple), and #257 Tibetan Blue (ice blue).

Weft
Bulky singles in a wool/mohair/cashmere blend (1,097 yd [1,003 m]/lb): 27 yd (24.5 m) dark purple, 50 yd (45.5 m) light purple, and 30 yd (27.5 m) ice blue (7 yd [6.5 m] included here for whipstitching selvedges and hemstitching ends). Additional yarn will be needed for sampling.
Shown here: Harrisville Designs Orchid Yarns (70% fine wool, 25% mohair, 5% cashmere; 1,097 yd [1,003 m]/lb): #255 Amethyst (dark purple), #256 Wisteria (light purple), and #257 Tibetan Blue (ice blue).

PROJECT NOTES

Weaving Plaid

Plaids require a lot of color changes (see page 30). Because there are an odd number of picks in each weft stripe, each stripe will end on the opposite side from where it started. When starting a new weft, be sure to start on the opposite side of the previous tucked tail to evenly distribute the extra bulk caused by the tucked tails.

Selvedge Treatment

To mask messy selvedges and visually balance the colors in the plaid, use ice blue threaded on a tapestry needle to whipstitch (see page 121) along each selvedge. For simplicity, thread 3 yards of ice blue on each of two tapestry needles. Using one needle at each selvedge, stop to work whipstitches along the edges after every few inches of cloth have been woven.

WARPING

Wind each color of warp separately.

Warp the loom (see page 24), following the specifications on page 65.

WEAVING

Weave an inch or two of header to spread the warp ends (see page 40).

Weave a sample to determine the degree of fulling you want. Leave 4" (10 cm) of unwoven warp between the sample and the beginning of the scarf.

Leave a 5" (12.5 cm) weft tail at the selvedge, then using a soft beat, weave one pick. Change sheds, tuck the 5" (12.5 cm) tail into the shed, allowing 1" (2.5 cm) to poke out. Weave another pick in the same shed and beat. Continue weaving a few inches with weft yarn according to the weft color order on page 65, adding whipstitches of ice blue along each selvedge (going around one warp and two wefts) as you go. Thread 25" (63.5 cm) of ice blue on a tapestry needle and use it to hemstitch (see page 120) around two warps and two wefts at the starting end of the scarf. Continue to weave and add whipstitches along the selvedges until the scarf measures 61" (155 cm; to produce a finished length of about 53" [134.5 cm]), ending at the right selvedge. Cut the weft, leaving an 6" (15 cm) tail. Needle weave (see page 120) this end back into the cloth. Thread 25" (63.5 cm) of ice blue on a tapestry needle and use it to hemstitch as before.

FINISHING

Remove the fabric from the loom (see page 46). Remove the scrap yarn in the header. With sharp scissors, cut the sample section from the fabric.

Fulling

Full (see page 55) the sample to the desired thickness, then full the scarf to match. Allow the fabric to thoroughly air-dry.

Trim the fringe to 2" (5 cm) using a rotary cutter on a self-healing mat.

two-skein **scarf**

the trick to weaving with variegated yarns is to use them in such a way as to bring out their beauty without combining too many colors so that they end up looking muddy. One trick is to grab a skein of beautifully variegated yarn and find a coordinating solid that will complement the variegated colorway, as in this scarf of subtle beauty. Simple hemstitching allows the variegated yarn to show in the fringe. For a different look, use the solid color in the warp and weave with the variegated.

Finished Dimensions
About 9" (23 cm) wide by 58½" (148.5 cm) long, plus 6" (15 cm) fringe at each end.

Weave Structure
Plain weave.

Equipment
10-dent rigid heddle with 10" (25.5 cm) weaving width; one stick shuttle.

Warp and Weft Specifications

Sett (epi)
10.

Weaving Width
10" (25.5 cm).

Picks per inch (ppi)
8.

Warp Length
90" (229 cm; includes 20" [51 cm] for loom waste and take-up; this does not allow for sampling).

Number of Warp Ends
100.

Yarns

Warp
4-ply wool/silk blend (1,150 yd [1,051.5 m]/lb): 250 yd (228.5 m) variegated. *Shown here:* Mountain Colors Twizzle (85% merino, 15% silk; 1,142 yd [1,044 m]/lb): Indian Corn.

Weft
2-ply alpaca/wool/metallic blend (1,250 yd [1,143 m]/lb): 135 yd teal. *Shown here:* Nashua Handknits Ivy (50% alpaca, 45% merino, 5% estellina; 1,252 yd [1,145 m]/lb): Blue Teal.

WARPING

Warp the loom (see page 24), following the specifications on page 69.

WEAVING

Weave an inch or two of header to spread the warp ends (see page 40).

Leave a 30" (76 cm) weft tail at the selvedge to use for hemstitching later, then using a soft beat, weave a few inches with weft yarn. Thread the weft tail on a tapestry needle and use it to hemstitch (see page 120) around two warps and two wefts at the starting end of the scarf. Continue to weave until the scarf measures 60" (152.5 cm). Cut the weft, leaving a 30" (76 cm) tail. Thread the tail on a tapestry needle and use it to hemstitch as before.

FINISHING

Remove the fabric from the loom (see page 46), using the loom waste for fringe. Remove the scrap yarn in the header.

Handwash in lukewarm water with mild soap, rinse. Roll in a towel and squeeze out excess water. Lay flat to dry. Trim the fringe to 6" (15 cm) using a rotary cutter on a self-healing mat.

what is a variegated yarn?

I've seen the term "variegated" applied to yarns that are simply multicolored (for instance, two different colors plied together). "Variegated" refers to a yarn that has repeating bands of color along the length of the yarn. There are a bevy of beautiful handpainted, variegated yarns on the market. When you weave with these yarns in the weft, "pooling" occurs if the bands of color stack upon one another. It is all too easy to lose the great colors when a variegated weft yarn interlaces with the warp yarn. Use the tips in the Two-Skein Scarf on page 69 and Piping Hot Pillows on page 73 to weave with these yarns for smashing results.

piping hot **pillows**

weaving with variegated yarns mean that you can get lots of patterning and color with very little effort, if you pick your colors right. These two pillows show three ways to weave with variegated yarns—variegated as warp, variegated as weft, and variegated as warp and weft. The fabric is sewn into a square and stuffed with a commercial pillow form. The pillows are neatly finished with a loom-woven tubular weave band piping. You could also embellish the pillows by stitching on lengths of tubular weave in free-form designs.

Finished Dimensions
About 14" square.

Weave Structure
Plain weave.

Equipment
8-dent rigid heddle with 16" weaving width; one stick shuttle; tapestry needle.

Warp and Weft Specifications

Sett (epi)
8.

Weaving Width
Pillow—15½".
Piping—1¼".

Picks per Inch (ppi)
Pillow—6.
Piping—3.

Warp Length
Each Pillow—64" (162.5 cm; includes 30" [76 cm] for loom waste and take-up).
Each Piping—86" (218 cm; includes 30" [76 cm] for loom waste and take-up).

Number of Warp Ends
Pillow—124.
Piping—10.

Yarns

Pillow Warp
Single-spun heavy worsted-weight wool (630 yd [576 m]/lb): 221 yd (202 m) red or variegated.
Shown here: Manos del Uruguay (100% wool; 630 yd [576 m]/lb): #69 red or #113 Wildflower.

Pillow Weft
Single-spun heavy worsted-weight wool (630 yd [576 m] /lb): 45 yd (41 m) each red and pastel variegated.
2-ply sportweight wool (1,700 yd [1554.5 m]/lb): 16 yd (14.5 m) red (for hem only).
Shown here: Manos del Uruguay (100% wool; 630 yd [576 m]/lb): #69 red and #113 Wildflower.
Brown Sheep Nature Spun Sport Weight (100% wool; 1,700 yd [1,554.5 m]/lb): #44 Husker Red.

Piping Warp
Single-spun heavy worsted-weight wool (630 yd [576 m]/lb): 24 yd (22 m) red or pastel variegated.
Shown here: Manos del Uruguay (100% wool; 630 yd [576 m]/lb): #69 red or #113 Wildflower.

Piping Weft
Single-spun heavy worsted-weight wool (630 yd [576 m]/lb): 7 yd (6.5 m) red or pastel variegated.
Shown here: Manos del Uruguay (100% wool; 630 yd [576 m]/lb): #69 red or #113 Wildflower.

Other Supplies
Coordinating sewing thread and sharp-point sewing needle; 14" x 14" (35.5 x 35.5 cm) pillow form (form shown by Eco Craft (cotton fabric stuffed with corn fiber); Fray Check (available at fabric and craft stores).

PROJECT NOTES

Although the warp is a bulky single-spun yarn, it holds up remarkably well under tension and can withstand a fair amount of abrasion without fraying.

Because this fabric has more warp ends per inch than weft picks, whichever yarn is in the warp will appear more dominant.

WARPING

Using the red warp for one pillow and the pastel variegated warp for the other, warp the loom (see page 24), following the specifications on page 73.

Wind three stick shuttles: one with bulky red, one with bulky variegated, and one with fingering-weight wool.

WEAVING THE PILLOW

Weave an inch or two with scrap yarn to spread the warp ends (see page 40).

Leave a 30" (76 cm) tail to use for hemstitching later, then using a soft beat, weave 1" (2.5 cm) with fingering-weight wool. Thread the weft tail on a tapestry needle and use it to hemstitch (see page 120) around two warps and wefts at the starting end of the scarf. Weave 16" (40.5 cm) with the variegated yarn, then switch to red and weave another 16" (40.5 cm), and finish by weaving 1" (2.5 cm) with the fingering-weight wool. Cut the weft, leaving a 30" (76 cm) tail. Thread the tail on a tapestry needle and use it to hemstitch as before.

FINISHING

Remove the fabric from the loom (see page 46). Remove the scrap yarn in the header.

WEAVING THE PIPING

Weave one piping with red warp and one piping with variegated warp. The piping is woven separately in a structure called tubular weave. To weave tubular weave, warp the loom with ten 86" (218.5 cm) warp ends. Wind a short stick shuttle with 2½ yards (2.3 meters) of weft yarn. Leave a 6" (15 cm) weft tail at the right selvedge if you're right-handed or at the left selvedge if you're left-handed to use to cinch the end, then pass the shuttle through the shed. Change the shed without bringing the reed to the fell of the cloth. Bring the shuttle under the warp and back to the same side where it entered the shed before. Pass the shuttle through the new shed. Holding the shuttle in your palm, pinch the exiting yarn between your thumb and index finger about 2" (5 cm) from the selvedge, tug firmly downward on the weft yarn to move it into place. Take care to not pinch the yarn too far from the shed and exert too much pressure, as singles yarn has a tendency to pull apart. Continue weaving in this manner for a few inches, always entering the shed from the same side so that the narrow warp forms a tube. Make several half-hitch knots with the weft to cinch the end of the piping. Continuing weaving until the tube measures 56" (142 cm) long (you will lose about 17% of the length due to take-up and shrinkage once it is washed).

FINISHING

Full (see page 55) the pillow and piping fabric in the washing machine set for a gentle cycle with mild soap and warm water or handwash the fabric using warm water and mild soap. If handwashing, gently agitate the cloth for a few minutes to encourage the fabric to full, then gently squeeze out the water by wrapping the fabric in a towel. With either method, lay the fabric flat to air-dry. Trim the fringe right up to the knot on the piping and the hemstitching on the pillow.

weaving tubular weave

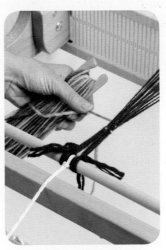

1. Pass the shuttle through the shed, leaving a 6" (15 cm) tail at the selvedge.

2. Change the shed and bring the shuttle under warp and around to same side it previously entered.

3. Pass the shuttle through the new shed, then tug downward on the weft to tighten the piping.

4. Tie the weft tail in the second half hitch to cinch the end of the piping.

Assembly

Fold the 1" (2.5 cm) of fabric woven with the fingering yarn to the wrong side of the pillow fabric and, using sewing thread, whipstitch (see page 121) it in place to form a hem. Repeat on the other end. Fold the cloth in half so that the seams are facing out. Using a tapestry needle and the thin weft, work a baseball stitch (see page 120) under the first thick pick to assure that the seam is hidden when sewn, then sew the two ends together. Sew one of the sides to form an envelope. Turn the fabric right side out and place the pillow form inside the fabric envelope. Fold the remaining open side down inside the pillow about 1" (2.5 cm) and sew the fabric together close to the edge of pillow form.

Place the knotted end of piping at the center of one side of the sewn pillow. Using coordinating sewing thread, use whipstitches to sew the base of the piping to the pillow seam. Sew the piping around all four sides. Cut the piping so that the end just covers the knot where you began, seal the cut with Fray Check, and sew the sealed end over the knot.

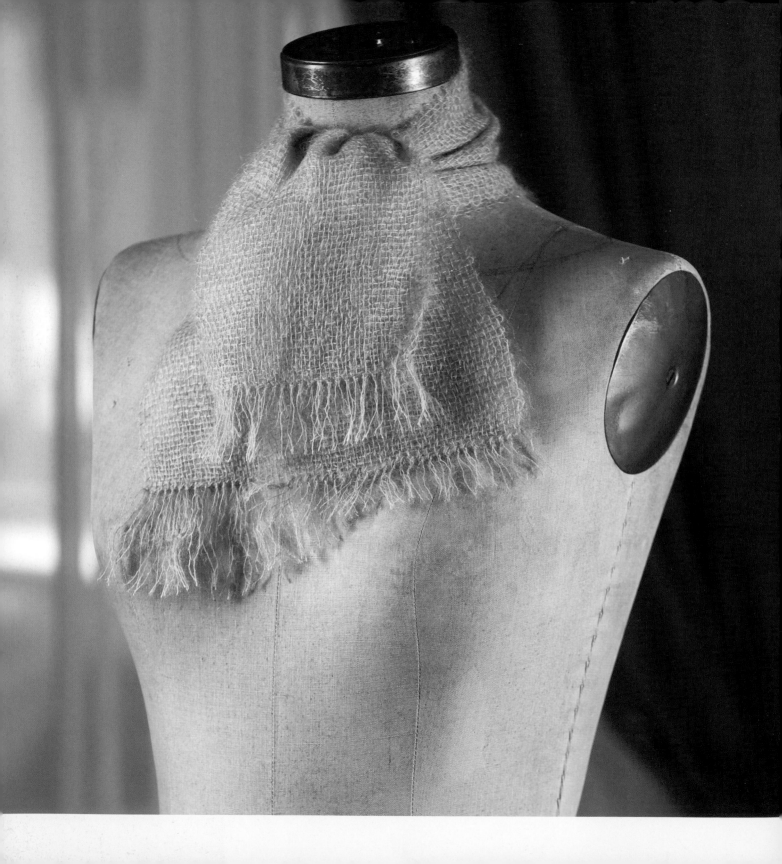

layered cravat

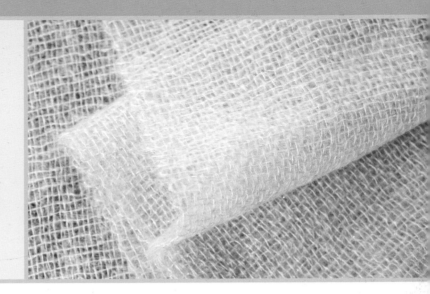

short decorative scarves tied snuggly at the nape of the neck provide an elegant touch to your day. Usually thought of as a man's accessory, this two-layered interpretation weaves up quickly and uses very little yarn, allowing you to freely use luxury yarns with smashing results. A blend of fine kid mohair was used in both the warp and weft on this cravat. Although mohair is a sticky yarn that can be tricky when used as a warp, the loose sett used here helps alleviate the problem. The yarns in the two layers shown here are close in hue, but one has a dash of metallic for a subtle sparkle.

Finished Dimensions
2 scarves, each about 6" (15 cm) wide by 33" (84 cm) long, plus 1" (2.5 cm) fringe at each end.

Weave Structure
Plain weave.

Equipment
10-dent rigid heddle with 6" (15 cm) weaving width; two stick shuttles.

Warp and Weft Specifications

Sett (epi)
10.

Weaving Width
6" (15 cm).

Picks per Inch (ppi)
8.

Warp Length
98" (249 cm; includes 30" [76 cm] for loom waste and take-up).

Number of Warp Ends
60.

Yarns

Warp
2-ply laceweight kid mohair/merino wool/microfiber blend (5,000 yd [4,572 m]/lb): 165 yd (151 m) light blue (#4681).
Shown here: Crystal Palace Kid Merino (28% kid mohair, 28% merino wool, 44% microfiber; 240 yd [219.5 m]/25 g): #4681 Misty Blue (light blue).

Weft
2-ply laceweight kid mohair/silk/polyester/nylon blend (4,700 yd [4,295.5 m]/lb): 49 yd (45 m) gray.
2-ply laceweight kid mohair/merino wool/microfiber blend (5,000 yd [4,572 m]/lb): 46 yd (42 m) light blue.
Shown here: Rowan Kidsilk Night (67% kid mohair, 18% silk, 10% polyester, 5% nylon; 227 yd [207.5 m]/25 g): #608 Moonlight (gray). Crystal Palace Kid Merino (28% kid mohair, 28% merino wool, 44% microfiber; 240 yd [219.5 m]/25 g): #4681 Misty Blue (light blue).

WARPING

Wind each weft color separately on a stick shuttle.

Warp the loom (see page 24), following the specifications on page 77.

WEAVING

Weave under moderate tension so as not to break the fine threads and use a soft hand when beating in the weft shots. Weave an inch or two header to spread the warp ends (see page 40). Leaving a 30" (76 cm) tail to use for hemstitching later, with gray, weave 1" (2.5 cm). Thread the weft tail on a tapestry needle and use it to hemstitch (see page 120) around two warps and two wefts at the starting end of the scarf. Weave 34" (86.5 cm), ending at the right selvedge. Cut the weft, leaving a 30" (76 cm) tail. Thread the tail on a tapestry needle and use it to hem-stitch as before.

Advance the warp so that there is a 4" (10 cm) gap from the end of the first scarf, then repeat the process with light blue for the second scarf.

FINISHING

Remove the fabric from the loom (see page 46), leaving at least 2" (5 cm) loom waste at each end for fringe. Remove the waste yarn from the header. With sharp scissors, cut the two scarf sections apart in the center of the 4" (10 cm) gap between the woven sections. Washing is not necessary. Trim the fringe on each end of each scarf to 1" (2.5 cm) with a rotary cutter against a self-healing mat.

tweed **so fine**

weaving fine fabrics on the rigid heddle loom is simply a matter of doubling or tripling fine yarns to create beautiful basketweave fabric. This type of fabric practically spills off the loom. Basketweave is formed when groups of two or more wefts weave under and over equal groups of two or more warps. In this scarf, three ends of a fingering-weight wool-silk yarn are used as a single warp end and weft pick. Using a combination of mossy colors creates a sophisticated masculine look.

Finished Dimensions
About 5¼" (13.5 cm) wide by 64" (162.5 cm) long, plus 4½" (11.5 cm) fringe at each end.

Weave Structure
Basketweave.

Equipment
8-dent rigid heddle with 6" (15 cm) weaving width; one stick shuttle.

Warp and Weft Specifications

Sett (epi)
8.

Weaving Width
6" (15 cm).

Picks per Inch (ppi)
10.

Warp Length
100" (256 cm; includes 30" [76 cm] for loom waste and take-up; 9" [23 cm] of the loom waste is used for fringe).

Number of Warp Ends
48 (using three ends as one).

Yarns

Warp
2-ply fingering-weight wool/silk blend (5,040 yd [4,608.5 m]/lb): 134 yd (122.5 m) each of tan, forest green, and blue.
Shown here: Jaggerspun 2/18 Zephyr Wool/Silk (50% wool, 50% silk; 5,040 yd [4,608.5 m]): Suede (tan), Bottle Green (forest green), and Marine Blue (blue).

Weft
2/18 fingering-weight wool/silk blend (5,040 yd [4,608.5 m]/lb): 130 yd (119 m) each of tan, forest green, and blue.
Shown here: Jaggerspun 2/18 Zephyr Wool/Silk (50% wool, 50% silk; 5,040 yd [4,608.5 m]/lb): Suede (tan), Bottle Green (forest green), and Marine Blue (blue).

WARPING

Place each cone or ball of yarn in a container to keep the warp from tangling while winding the warp and stick shuttle. Use the three yarns together as one.

Warp the loom (see page 24) according to the specifications on page 81. The loom waste will be used for fringe so be sure to allow 4½" (11.5 cm) of warp length when tying the warp onto the front apron rod.

WEAVING

Weave an inch or two with scrap yarn to spread the warp ends (see page 40). Leaving a 30" (76 cm) tail to use for hemstitching later, weave for 1" (2.5 cm). Thread the weft tail on a tapestry needle and use it to hemstitch (see page 120) around two warps and wefts at the starting end of the scarf. Weave 69" (175 cm) more, then cut the weft, leaving a 30" (76 cm) tail. Thread the tail on a tapestry needle and use it to hemstitch as before.

FINISHING

Remove the fabric from the loom (see page 46), leaving at least 4½" (11.5 cm) of loom waste at each end for fringe. Remove the scrap yarn in the header.

Handwash with delicate soap, then rinse. Roll the piece in a towel to remove excess moisture, then lay flat to dry. Trim fringe to 4" (10 cm) by hand or with a rotary cutter.

WARPING

Wind each color of warp separately.

Warp the loom (see page 24) according to the specifications on page 85 and starting and ending with red warp ends.

Wind each color on a separate shuttle.

WEAVING

Weave an inch or two of header to spread the warp ends (see page 40).

Leaving a 24" (61 cm) tail at the selvedge to use for hemstitching later, weave two picks of red. Starting the brown from the same side as the red exited, but in a different shed, weave two picks of brown. Pick up the red shuttle from under the brown thread so that it catches neatly at the edge (see Managing Two Shuttles, page 45), and weave two picks with red. Do the same with the brown. Thread the red weft tail on a tapestry needle and use it to hemstitch (see page 120) around two warps and two wefts at the beginning of the piece.

Continue alternating two picks each of red and brown until the cloth measures 25" (63.5 cm; it doesn't matter which color you end with). Cut the weft, leaving a 24" (61 cm) tail. Thread the tail on a tapestry needle and use it to hemstitch as before. Cut the other weft yarn and needle-weave (see page 120) the end back into the cloth.

Advance the warp, leaving 1" (2.5 cm) of unwoven warp. Weave a second section of cloth measuring 72" (183 cm) long, hemstitched at both ends as before.

FINISHING

Remove the fabric from the loom (see page 46). Remove the scrap yarn in the header. With sharp scissors, cut apart the two pieces. Machine wash with mild soap and allow to air-dry.

Trim the fringe ¼" (6 mm) from the hemstitching.

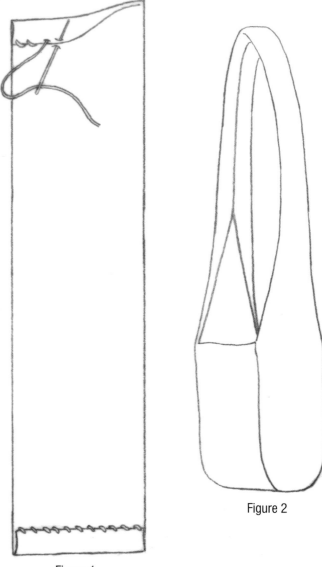

Figure 1

Figure 2

ASSEMBLY

Fold over each end of the shorter piece ¼" (6 mm) two times for hem, hiding the hemstitching. With red, use a whipstitch (see page 121) to sew the hem in place (Figure 1). Repeat for both sides of the longer fabric.

Fold the shorter body fabric in half widthwise with the hem facing inward. Fold the long piece of cloth for the strap. Align each end of the strap with the fold in the body cloth and tuck two picks (one strip of red) of the strap

Figure 3

under the body fabric to form a seam allowance, making sure that the pattern is aligned across the entire fabric. With red, sew the two pieces together. Repeat for the other side, taking care not to twist the strap (Figure 2).

Using a whipstitch, sew the two selvedge edges of the strap together on the underside of the strap, beginning and ending 3" from the bag body. Allow the edges of the strap to taper to full width at the top of the bag and stitch in place (Figure 3).

To form a flat base, push the sewn ends of the strap into points, then fold the points so that they butt up against the side seams and stitch in place.

color and weave

Dozens of patterns can be created by clever combinations of light and dark yarns in the warp and weft. The patterns show up best if there is high contrast between the light and dark yarns. Color with low contrast will create interesting effects, but they won't be as sharply defined.

In the sampler shown here, two ends of purples are alternated with two ends of mint green in the warp. The first square is woven by alternating one pick each of purple and green. The second square is woven by alternating two picks each of purple and green. The third square is woven with all purple weft. The fourth is woven with all green weft. Use your imagination to come up with other combinations in both the warp and weft!

pleasing proportions **bag**

modern art and Scandinavian design offers endless inspiration for weaving. In both disciplines proportional blocks are utilized beautifully. Tapestry, a weft-faced plain-weave technique, is a great way to place pure color blocks next to one another. Only the weft yarn shows in tapestry (there are no visible interactions between the warp and weft), which makes it easier to choose harmonizing colors. The only trick is to be consistent in how the two colors are handled at the color changes. In this project, the green always lays on top of the brown at the join.

Finished Dimensions

About 7" (18 cm) wide by 8½" (21.5 cm) long, with 42" (106.5 cm) strap.

Weave Structure

Weft-faced tapestry.

Equipment

12-dent rigid heddle with a 7" (18 cm) weaving width; two 8" (20.5 cm) stick shuttles; two 6" (15 cm) stick shuttles; tapestry beater or fork (optional).

Warp and Weft Specifications

Sett (epi)
4 (using a 12-dent rigid heddle).

Weaving Width
7" (18 cm).

Picks per Inch (ppi)
34.

Warp Length
60" (152 cm; includes 30" [76 cm] for loom waste and take-up, and 10" [25.5 cm] for sampling).

Number of Warp Ends
28.

Yarns

Warp
2-ply worsted-weight wool (900 yd [823 m]/lb): 47 yd (43 m) olive green.
Shown here: Harrisville Design Highland (100% wool; 450 yd [411.5 m]/8 oz): Cypress (olive green).

Weft
2-ply worsted-weight wool (900 yd [823 m]/lb): 60 yd (55 m) olive green, 15 yd (13.5 m) forest green, 9 yd (8 m) brown, and 39 yd (35.5 m) brick red. Additional yarn will be needed for sampling.
Shown here: Harrisville Design Highland (100% wool; 450 yd [411.5 m]/8 oz):
Cypress (olive green), Evergreen (forest green), Teak (brown), and Russet (brick red).

Strap
60" (152.5 cm) of ⅛" (3 mm) tan leather cord.
2-ply worsted-weight wool (900 yd [823 m]/lb): 8 yd (7.5 m) each forest green, brown, and brick red.
Shown here: Harrisville Design Highland (100% wool; 450 yd [411.5 m]/8 oz): Evergreen (forest green), Teak (brown), and Russet (brick red).

bamboo **obi**

the obi is the outermost sash worn with a Japanese kimono. Typically it is quite long and wraps around the body several times. This modernized version uses a color reversal so that you see two different patterns as it wraps around the body. The warp-faced fabric is stiff enough to hold its shape, while the bamboo provides drape and sheen. The patterning is a result of alternating dark and light threads in the warp and weft. Long twisted fringe provides an elegant finished look that enables a knot to be tied without wrinkling the cloth.

Finished Dimensions
About 3¾" (9.5 cm) wide by 62" (157.5 cm) long, with 10½" (26.5 cm) fringe at each end.

Weave Structure
Warp-faced plain weave.

Equipment
12-dent rigid heddle with 4" (10 cm) weaving width; one 4" (10 cm) belt or inkle (beveled-edge) shuttle.

Warp and Weft Specifications

Sett (epi)
12.

Weaving Width
6¾" (17 cm).

Picks per Inch (ppi)
10.

Warp Length
124" (315 cm; includes 30" [76 cm] for loom waste and take-up, and 10" [25.5 cm] for sampling).

Number of Warp Ends
81.

Warp Color Order
[1 light, 2 dark, 3 light, 5 dark, 3 light, 2 dark] 5 times, end 1 light.

Yarns

Warp
4-ply light worsted-weight (DK) bamboo (1,050 yd [960 m]/lb): 124 yd light green, 155 yd (142 m) dark green.
Shown here: Halcyon Yarn Satin Bamboo (100% bamboo; 200 yd [183 m]/3 oz): #23 (light green) and #24 (dark green).

Weft
4-ply light worsted-weight (DK) bamboo (1,050 yd [960 m]/lb): 42 yd (38.5 m) light green and 42 (38.5 m) yd dark green. Additional yarn will be needed for sampling.
Shown here: Halcyon Yarn Satin Bamboo (100% bamboo; 200 yd [183 m]/3 oz): #23 (light green) and #24 (dark green).

PROJECT NOTES

The trick to weaving warp-faced fabric is to use a firm consistent beat that will maintain the cloth's width evenly throughout the weaving process. Use a belt or inkle shuttle that has a beveled edge and that is about the width of your fabric. Instead of beating with the rigid heddle, use the shuttle to press the weft into place. Use the 10" (25.5 cm) of sampling warp to practice your beat.

Pack as much yarn on the shuttle as you can (ideally the entire length of this weft) without interfering with the warp as you weave—joins in warp-faced fabrics are more likely to show. If you can't get all of the yarn on the smaller shuttle, consider using a larger shuttle.

WARPING

Warp the loom (see page 24) following the specifications on page 93.

Wind the dark green on the shuttle, leaving the beveled edge free of yarn (see page 106).

WEAVING

Sampling

Because this is a warp-faced fabric, there's no need to use scrap yarn to spread the warp. Instead, you want the warp to spread as little as possible. In the first shed, bring the yarn to just the point where the warp begins to show gaps from being tied onto the apron rod. Change sheds without bringing the rigid heddle forward, use the sharp edge of the shuttle to press the weft yarn into place. Continue by throwing a pick, changing sheds without bringing the rigid heddle to the fell of the cloth, then pressing the yarn into place. Place the weft at an angle of about 20 degrees (the warp will do most of the bending in the under-over sequence, not the weft). Change sheds, again without bringing the reed to the fell. Then use the sharp edge of the shuttle to press the weft firmly into place. Practice for the length of your sample warp to achieve even tension and straight selvedges.

Advance the warp, leaving a 12" (30.5 cm) gap between the sample and the beginning of the belt fabric (this will be used for fringe). Insert two shots of fine scrap yarn to hold the bamboo picks in place when you cut the cloth from the loom.

Begin weaving with dark green for 31" (78.5 cm) maintaining a firm and even beat. Check the width often and unweave picks as necessary if the width changes. Change to light green and weave for 31" (78.5 cm) more. Finish by weaving another two picks with fine scrap yarn.

FINISHING

Remove the fabric from the loom (see page 46), leaving 12" (30.5 cm) of loom waste at each end for fringe. Remove the two picks of scrap yarn.

Fringe

Using two groups of two warp ends at a time, make twisted fringe (see page 121) along each short end of the obi. Tie an overhand knot about 2" (5 cm) from the end of each twisted fringe, taking care to make the knots all the same distance from the cloth. Trim the ends evenly.

It isn't necessary to wash the belt before wearing. When it is time to launder, handwash the belt in lukewarm water with gentle soap. Rinse, then roll in a towel to remove excess moisture. Lay flat to dry.

MAKING THE WEFT

The weft is made by joining cotton loopers into a chain as shown below.

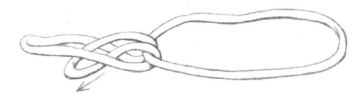

Blue Mat

Connect the two shades of blue loopers in the following order: [1 aqua, 4 light blue, 1 aqua, 1 light blue] 24 times. Make another two strands of loopers connected as 1 orange, 1 pink, 4 orange.

Orange and Pink Mat

Connect the orange and pink loopers in the following order: [1 pink, 4 orange, 1 pink, 1 orange] 24 times. Make another two strands of loopers connected as 1 light blue, 1 aqua, 4 light blue.

PROJECT NOTES

Ski shuttles are better than stick shuttles for bulky wefts such as the loopers. Wind the shuttle in wide figure eights.

getting a firm beat

A firm beat is critical for a sturdy mat. For each pick, place the weft in the first shed, bring the rigid heddle to the fell of the cloth, change the shed by pulling up or pushing down the rigid heddle, then move the rigid heddle back into the shed blocks. Use a heavy tapestry beater to press the weft firmly into place.

WARPING

Warp the loom (see page 24) following the specifications on page 97.

WEAVING

Wind light green carpet warp on one stick shuttle. Wind two short strands of orange and pink loopers on another stick shuttle. Wind the blue loopers on a ski shuttle, forming a wide figure eight.

Weave an inch or two of header to spread the warp ends (see page 40).

Leaving a 30" (76 cm) tail at the selvedge, weave 1" (2.5 cm) with light green carpet warp for the hem. Thread the tail on a tapestry needle and use it to hemstitch (see page 120) around two warps and two wefts at the starting end of the mat. Weave four picks with the blue loopers. Separate the woven weft from the loose weft by detaching the last looper that sticks out from the shed.

To keep the color joins from being visually distracting, tuck the resulting blue tail back into the warp under the last pick. In the same shed, at the opposite end of the same shed, place half of an orange looper from one of the short strands. Beat. Weave two picks with short orange and pink strand. Weave 12½" (31.5 cm) with blue loopers. Weave two more picks of orange and pink. Weave four picks of blues. Weave 1" (2.5 cm) with carpet warp for hem. Hemstitch as before.

Place a 2" (5 cm) cardboard spacer after the hemstitching. Work a second mat after the cardboard spacer, reversing the colors.

FINISHING

Remove the fabric from the loom (see page 46). Remove the scrap yarn in the header.

Trim the warp to about ¼" (6 mm) from the hemstitching. Fold each hem in half and whipstitch (see page 121) in place on the wrong side.

space-saving **mats**

at times, being spacey can be a good thing. The spaces in these mats are formed by skipping holes and slots while the warp is threaded through the rigid heddle to create a lacy look while economizing on warp yarn. All four of these mats are woven on the same warp, but a different hue is used for the weft of each for visual variety. To keep the yarns from slipping, the first and last weft picks held in place with Fray Check, requiring no further finishing than trimming the fringe.

Finished Dimensions
Four mats, each about 14" (35.5 cm) wide by 19" (48.5 cm) long, with 2" (5 cm) fringe at each end.

Weave Structure
Plain weave with spaced warp.

Equipment
10-dent rigid heddle with 15" (38 cm) weaving width; one stick shuttle; three 4" (10 cm) cardboard spacers a little longer than the weaving width.

Warp and Weft Specifications
Sett (epi)
10.

Weaving Width
15" (38 cm).

Picks per Inch
10.

Warp Length
122" (310 cm; includes 30" [76 cm] for loom waste and take-up, and 4" [10 cm] between mats for fringe).

Number of Warp Ends
84.

Warp Spacing Order
[Thread 6, skip 12, thread 6, skip 3, thread 12, skip 3] 3 times, thread 6, skip 12, thread 6.

Yarns
Warp
2-ply 3/2 mercerized cotton (1,260 yd [1,152 m]/lb): 285 yd [260.5 m] yellow gold. *Shown here:* UKI 3/2 Mercerized Cotton Yarn (100% cotton; 1,260 yd [1,152 m]/lb): #30 Antique.

Weft
2-ply 3/2 mercerized cotton (1,260 yd [1,152 m]/lb): 92 yd (84 m) each of four shades of gold.
Shown here: UKI 3/2 Mercerized Cotton Yarn (100% cotton; 1,260 yd [1,152 m]/lb): #84 Gold Dust, #9 Ginger, #7 Oak, and #29 Old Gold.

Other Supplies
Fray Check.

leno **runner**

linen and leno are a natural combination. Linen, which comes from stiff plant fibers derived from the flax plant, provides a crisp finished look and high sheen. Fabrics woven from this fiber are called "linens." Leno is a form of lace where crossed warp threads are held in place by the weft. Use your fingers to cross the threads, then hold them in place with a pick-up stick while the weft is thrown to secure them in position. Simple to do, leno adds a decorative look to simple fabrics. The more rows of leno you work, the lacier the look.

Finished Dimensions
About 10¼" (26 cm) wide by 35" (89 cm) long, with 2" (5 cm) fringe at each end.

Weave Structure
Balanced plain weave with leno.

Equipment
10-dent rigid heddle with 11" (28 cm) weaving width; one stick shuttle; one pick-up stick.

Warp and Weft Specifications

Sett (epi)
10.

Weaving Width
10¾" (27.5 cm).

Picks per Inch (ppi)
6.

Warp Length
53" (134.5 cm; includes 24" [61 cm] for loom waste and take-up). *Note:* The loom waste is calculated as fringe to allow just one skein for the warp.

Number of Warp Ends
108.

Yarns

Warp
Worsted-weight wet-spun linen (870 yd [795.5 m]/lb): 190 yd (173.5 m) red. *Shown here:* Louet North America Euroflax Wet-Spun Linen (100% linen; 190 yd [173.5 m]/100 g): #11 Red.

Weft
Worsted-weight wet-spun linen (870 yd [795.5 m]/lb): 80 yd (73 m) berry red. *Shown here:* Louet North America Euroflax Wet-Spun Linen (100% linen; 70 yd [64 m]/100 g): #23 Berry Red.

brooks bouquet **shawl**

worked by wrapping weft around groups of warp threads, brooks bouquet creates a lovely lace pattern on plain-weave fabric. In this shawl, a small shuttle is used to wrap the weft around groups of eight warp ends after every five picks of plain weave are woven. The result is a honeycomb-type texture that looks much more complicated than it really is. The key to making beautiful fabric is to maintain constant tension in the weft. Combine this technique with soft luxury yarns to create a stunning wrap for chilly evenings.

Finished Dimensions
About 15" (38 cm) wide by 68" (173 cm) long, with 6½" (16.5 cm) fringe at each end.

Weave Structure
Balanced plain weave with brooks bouquet.

Equipment
10-dent rigid heddle with 20" (51 cm) weaving width; one 18" (45.5 cm) stick shuttle; one 4" (10 cm) stick shuttle.

Warp and Weft Specifications

Sett (epi)
10.

Weaving Width
20" (51 cm).

Picks per Inch (ppi)
6.

Warp Length
114" (290 cm; includes 30" [76 cm] for loom waste and take-up).

Number of Warp Threads
200.

Yarns

Warp
4-ply worsted-weight wool/microfiber acrylic/cashmere blend (896 yd [819 m]/lb): 634 yd (580 m) olive green.
Shown here: Cascade Yarns Cash Vero (55% merino, 33% microfiber acrylic, 12% cashmere; 98 yd [89.5 m]/50 g): #031 olive green.

Weft
4-ply worsted-weight wool/microfiber acrylic/cashmere blend (896 yd [819 m]/lb): 318 yd (291 m) olive green.
Shown here: Cascade Yarns Cash Vero (55% merino, 33% microfiber acrylic, 12% cashmere; 98 yd [89.5 m]/50 g): #031 olive green.

illustrated techniques

BASEBALL STITCH

Thread seaming yarn on a tapestry needle. Butt the selvedge edges of two pieces of fabric together or place them back to back. Working from bottom to top, *bring threaded needle from back to front near the edge of one side, then from back to front near the edge of the other side. Repeat from *, inserting the needle a short distance above the previous path.

BUTTONHOLE STITCH

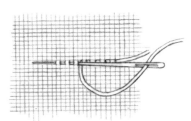

Thread stitching yarn on a tapestry needle. Working from right to left, *bring under the edge of the cloth to be covered, then out again a short distance away, being careful to bring the needle out on top of the stitching yarn. Repeat from * for the desired length.

HEMSTITCHING

Thread weft yarn on a tapestry needle. Working from right to left, *bring the threaded needle under the desired number of warp ends (two shown here) above the fell, then back to the starting point, encircling the group. Pass the needle under the same group of ends, bringing it out through the weaving the desired

number of weft picks below the fell (two shown here). Repeat from * across the fell. To end, needle weave the tail into the cloth and trim the end.

NEEDLE WEAVING

Thread the yarn to be needle-woven on a tapestry needle. Bring the needle in and out of the woven cloth, mimicking the over-under path of one warp end (if working vertically) or one weft pick (if working horizontally) in the woven cloth.

THREE-STRAND BRAID

Cut three strands (or three groups of strands) about two times the desired finished length. Tie the strands together at one end in an overhand knot. *Lay the right strand over the middle strand so that the right strand is now the middle strand. Lay the left strand over the new middle strand. Repeat from * to the desired length.

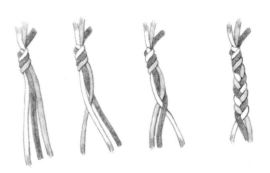

TWISTED FRINGE

Divide the number of strands for each fringe into two groups. Twist each group clockwise until it kinks. Bring both groups together and twist them counterclockwise (allow them to untwist around each other in that direction). Secure the ends with an overhand knot to prevent untwisting.

WHIPSTITCH

Thread seaming yarn on a tapestry needle. Hold the pieces to be seamed together with their wrong sides facing together. *Bring threaded needle through both layers from back to front. Repeat from *, inserting the needle a short distance above the previous path.

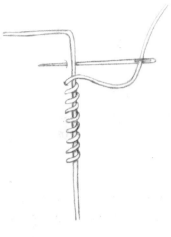

project planning cards

Photocopy this page and keep record of your projects on these handy cards.

PROJECT_____

Warp yarn and length _____

Weft yarn and length _____

Sett _____ Width in the reed _____ PPI _____

Woven dimensions off loom _____
After washing _____

Finishing Techniques _____

PROJECT_____

Warp yarn and length _____

Weft yarn and length _____

Sett _____ Width in the reed _____ PPI _____

Woven dimensions off loom _____
After washing _____

Finishing Techniques _____

terms to know

"Language is the source of misunderstandings."
— *Antoine de Saint Exupery*

One of the biggest challenges to learning anything new is mastering the language. This list will help you understand weaving lingo.

Advance the warp Release tension on the cloth and wind the woven cloth onto the front beam, then re-tension the warp to continue weaving.

Balanced plain weave or **balanced weave cloth** A fabric in which there is the same number of warp ends and weft picks per inch.

Beat Bring the rigid heddle to the fell of the cloth to align and pack the weft.

Beater Device used to position each weft pick. This is the same as the rigid heddle on a rigid heddle loom.

Bloom The expansion of yarn once washed and the fibers relax.

Choke tie Contrasting yarn tied around a bundle of warp ends to prevent them from slipping while the rigid heddle is threaded.

Count system Yarn classification system based on the number of yards in a pound of a standard size.

Cross Keeps the warp threads in order and minimizes tangles when threading the loom.

Dressing the loom The process of measuring the warp and winding it on the loom.

End (warp end) One strand of warp.

Ends per inch (epi) The number of warp threads in an inch.

Fell The part of the cloth where the weaving action occurs.

Felt To agitate scaled fibers so that they fuse together.

Float Where a weft pick doesn't travel in the normal over-under-over path.

Fringe The unwoven warp that is intentionally left at the ends of woven cloth.

Full Wash and agitate the fabric so that the yarn blooms, and in some cases, shrinks.

Grist The size of a yarn.

Hand The way the cloth feels.

Header The first inch or two of weaving (usually with scrap yarn) to spread out the warp ends to their full weaving width.

Heddles The molded plastic pieces in the rigid heddle through which the warp ends are threaded.

Hemstitching A way to secure the first and last weft picks of cloth (see page 120).

Leader yarn An inelastic yarn that marks the desired path to follow when measuring the warp on the warping board.

Loom waste The amount of extra yarn left over after weaving.

Pick (or shot) One pass of the shuttle through the shed.

Picks per inch (ppi) The number of weft picks in an inch of woven cloth.

Plain weave Cloth woven so that the weft picks alternate which warp ends they go over and under.

Plied yarn Yarn made up of two or more singles yarn.

Reed/rigid heddle In a shaft loom the reed is a separate piece of equipment. The rigid heddle loom incorporates both "rigid" heddles—they are loose on a shaft loom—and reed into one.

Reed stand An apparatus designed to hold the rigid heddle steady while the warp is threaded.

Selvedges The edge of the cloth where the weft exits one shed and enters the next.

Sett The spacing of the warp ends in the heddle.

Shed The open space that is created when the heddle is lifted up or down.

Shed blocks Used to hold the rigid heddle in the up or down position to produce a shed.

Shot See pick.

Shuttle Used to place the weft yarn in the shed.

Singles A single strand of spun fiber.

Stick shuttle A flat shuttle typically used when weaving on rigid heddle looms.

Take-up Extra inches of warp length needed to account for over-under path in the woven cloth.

Threads Used interchangeably with "yarn" to describe the warp or weft.

Throw To pass the shuttle into the shed.

Warp Threads held taught on a loom and the act of dressing the loom.

Warp dominant Cloth in which the warp ends completely cover the weft picks.

Warp-emphasis weave Cloth in which there are more warp ends per inch than weft picks.

Warp end An individual warp yarn or thread.

Warping board Device used to make it easy to measure the warp ends in preparation for threading the loom.

Weave The process of crossing taut warp threads with a weft thread in an over-under pattern.

Weft The yarn that is passed through the shed of a warped loom and beaten into place.

Weft dominant Cloth in which the weft picks completely cover the warp ends.

Weft-emphasis weave Cloth in which there are more weft picks per inch than warp ends.

Wraps per inch (wpi) The number of times a yarn can be wrapped around a rigid object in an inch.

warping checklist

Photocopy this page for each project and check off your progress.

WARPING CHECKLIST

Step One

- ❏ Place a leader string of a contrasting color on the warping board the length of the warp that you wish to wind.

- ❏ Wind the warp on warping board making a cross at each turn at the top.

- ❏ Tie a choke around the entire warp, except the leader string, with a two-foot long piece of yarn about two feet from the cross.

Step Two

- ❏ Secure the rigid heddle in a reed stand.

- ❏ Holding the cross in your left hand, take the warp to the rigid heddle.

- ❏ Cut top of the cross so that the threads hang individually.

- ❏ Thread the rigid heddle in the appropriate order.

Step Three

- ❏ Place the rigid heddle in the loom, making sure that the loose ends of the warp are facing the back beam.

- ❏ Tie the choke to the front beam.

- ❏ Tie the loose ends of the warp to the back apron rod in one-inch bundles.

- ❏ Cut the choke tie and wind the warp one rotation, securing heavy paper or sticks between the layers of threads.

- ❏ Wind for a few more rotations, then pull the warp with firm tension adding paper when necessary. Repeat until the end of the warp is pulled to the front beam.

- ❏ Tie the warp to the front apron rod in one-inch sections using a square knot. Adjust for even tension and secure the knots.

Your loom is warped. Weave on!

project planning sheet

Photocopy this page and keep record of your warp and weft calculations for every project.

PROJECT _____

Yarn Selection:
Wraps per inch _____ ÷ 2 = sett _____ (Note: If your heddle has ten dents per inch you want a yarn that wraps about twenty times per inch for balanced plain weave. *I recommend rounding up as you work.*)

Warp Length:
_____" (woven length of project) + 10% (take-up) = _____" + 24" (loom waste) = _____ + 10" (for sampling if desired) = _____" length of each warp thread.

Total Number of Warp Threads Needed:
_____" (woven width of project) + 10% (take-up) = _____" (width in the reed) × (number of ends per inch or sett) = _____ number of warp threads.

Amount of Yarn Needed for Warp:
_____ (number of warp threads) × _____" (warp length) = _____" ÷ 36 = _____' (the amount of yarn needed for warp in yards).

Amount of Yarn Needed for Weft:
_____" (width of warp in reed) + 10% (take-up) × _____ (picks per inch)= _____" × _____" (total length of woven warp) = _____ ÷ 36 = _____' (the amount of yarn needed for weft in yards).

Finishing technique _____

Yarn Sample _____ **Source** _____

Yarn Sample _____ **Source** _____

Yarn Sample _____ **Source** _____

Notes _____

sett chart

This list includes scans of each of the yarns used in *Weaving Made Easy*. Underneath each scan you will find the yards per pound (and meters per kilogram) along with a recommended sett for balanced plain weave. Keep in mind that some of the setts may differ from the way they are used in the projects if denser or looser setts were used to weave warp- or weft-emphasis or lacy fabrics. You can use the scans to compare yarns you have on hand and make substitutions. When substituting yarns, it is a good idea to use similar fiber types with the same yarn characteristics.

COTTON

4-ply bulky weight unmercerized cotton; 400 yd/lb (810 m/kg); 8

2-ply 3/2 mercerized (pearl) cotton; 1,260 yd/lb (2,444 m/kg); 10

2-ply 8/4 fingering-weight unmercerized cotton; 1,600 yd/lb (3,390 m/kg); 12

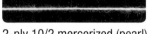

2-ply 10/2 mercerized (pearl) cotton; 4,000 yd/lb (8,475 m/kg); 24

WOOL

2-ply very bulky wool; 260 yd/lb (525 m/kg); 4

Heavy worsted-weight singles wool; 630 yd/lb (1,271 m/kg); 8

2-ply worsted-weight wool; 900 yd/lb (1,816 m/kg); 8

3-ply worsted-weight wool; 1,000 yd/lb (2,010 m/kg); 10

2-ply sportweight wool; 1,700 yd/lb (3,431 m/kg); 10

2-ply 28/2 fingering-weight wool; 2,240 yd/lb (4,520 m/kg); 15

BLENDS

2-ply alpaca/wool/metallic blend; 1,250 yd/lb (2,522 m/kg); 10

4-ply wool/silk blend; 1,150 yd/lb (2,230 m/kg);10

Bulky singles wool/mohair/cashmere blend; 1,097 yd/lb (2,213 m/kg); 10

4-ply worsted-weight wool/microfiber acrylic/cashmere blend; 896 yd/lb (1,808 m/kg); 10

2-ply lace-weight kid mohair/merino wool/microfiber blend; 5,000 yd/lb (10,100 m/kg); 10

2-ply 18/2 wool/silk blend; 5,040 yd/lb (10,170 m/kg); 24

OTHER FIBERS

4-ply light worsted-weight (DK) bamboo; 1,050 yd/lb (2,113 m/kg); 10

3-ply worsted-weight wet-spun linen; 870 yd/lb; (1,756 m/kg); 10

sources for supplies

SOURCES FOR YARNS

Companies with a * are wholesale only. Contact these companies for a retail source in your area.

*Brown Sheep Company
100662 County Rd. 16
Mitchell, NE 69375
brownsheep.com

*Cascade Yarns
PO Box 58168
1224 Andover Park East
Tukwila, WA 98188
cascadeyarns.com

Crystal Palace
160 23rd St.
Richmond, CA 94804
straw.com/cpy

Cotton Clouds
5176 S. Fourteenth Ave.
Safford, AZ 85546
cottonclouds.com
Superior Cotton Loopers

Diamond Yarn
9697 St. Laurent, Ste. 101
Montreal, QC
Canada H3L 2N1
diamondyarn.com

Halcyon Yarn
12 School St.
Bath, ME 04530
halcyonyarn.com

Harrisville Designs
Center Village
PO Box 806
Harrisville, NH 03450
harrisville.com

*JaggerSpun
PO Box 188
Springvale, ME 04083
jaggerspun.com

Louet North America
808 Commerce Park Dr.
Ogdensburg, NY 13669
louet.com
in Canada:
RR #4
Prescott, ON K0E 1T0

Lunatic Fringe
15009 Cromartie Rd.
Tallahassee, FL 32309
lunatic@talstar.com

*Design Source/Manos del Uruguay
PO Box 770
Medford, MA 02155

*Mountain Colors
PO Box 156
Corvallis, MT 59828
mountaincolors.com

*Westminster Fibers/ Nashua/Rowan
165 Ledge St.
Nashua, NH 03060
westminsterfibers.com
in Canada: Diamond Yarn

*Universal Yarns
284 Ann St.
Concord, NC 28025

*UKI
PO Box 848
Hickory, NC 28603

SOURCES FOR LOOMS

*Foxglove Fiberarts Supply/Ashford Looms
8040 NE Day Rd., Bldg. 4, Ste. F
Bainbridge Island, WA 98110
(877) 369-4568
foxglovefiber.com

Glimakra USA
50 Hall Ln.
Clancy, MT 59634
(866) 890-7314
glimakrausa.com

Harrisville Designs
PO Box 806
Harrisville, NH 03450
(603) 827-3333
harrisville.com

*Leclerc Looms
1573 Savoie C.P. 4
Plessisville, QC
Canada G6L 2Y6
(819) 362-2408
leclerclooms.com

*New Voyager Trading
PO Box 468
Murfreesboro, NC 27855
(252) 398-4396
newvoyager.com

*Schacht Spindle Co.
6101 Ben Pl.
Boulder, CO 80301
(303) 442-3212
schachtspindle.com